THE AMUSEMENT PARK AND WATERPARK INJURY GUIDE: NATIONAL EDITION

By Attorney Jill Ruane, Attorney Jay Ruane, and Attorney Seth Price

Edited by Jennifer Sanfilippo

Printed in the United States of America.
Different Middle Initial, LLC
ISBN: 978-1-7326411-0-5

TABLE OF CONTENTS

INTRODUCTION

Amusement parks, waterparks, carnivals, and fairs provide entertainment for the family year round. They are especially popular during the summer months, when the weather is warm, the kids are on vacation, and there are plenty of opportunities to enjoy family time. One great thing about these activities is that there is something for everyone! Between games, rides, and great food, everyone in the family will find something to enjoy.

Amusement parks, waterparks, fairs, and carnivals are filled with fun and excitement, but when your children are playing in the water, going on fast rides, or playing games, sometimes accidents can happen. This is what inspired us to create this book on park and carnival injuries. If you go to the amusement park intending to have a fun day, but your child gets injured, there is something you can do.

This book will give you helpful information on parks, carnivals, and fairs throughout the country, as well as what to do if something goes wrong at one of these locations. The first chapter talks about different types of venues where you might find amusement rides. The second chapter discusses popular amusement parks located in the United States. Chapter Three goes over common amusement park rides as well as ways that they could malfunction and cause danger to your family. Chapter Four goes over common injuries that a person might sustain on amusement park rides. Understanding these rides and potential dangers can help you keep your family safe, and can give you important information in case an accident does happen.

Chapters Five and Six focus on waterparks and their potential hazards. Chapter Five discusses common waterpark rides that you might encounter at a park. Then, Chapter Six goes through common waterpark injuries that might occur and affect your children.

Chapter Seven discusses carnivals, fairs, and festivals. It talks about common games and rides at these venues, and how to protect your children from accidents. Finally, Chapter Eight explains information about personal injury cases and legal terminology.

If your child has been injured at an amusement park, waterpark, fair, or carnival, you need to take action in order to protect them. Call our office as soon as possible to speak with an attorney about your family's situation.

CHAPTER 1: VENUES

Sometimes, it can be difficult to differentiate between amusement parks, waterparks, and other types of amusement venues. In this chapter, I define some popular terms, such as amusement parks, theme parks, fairs, festivals, carnivals, parks, and playgrounds. Understanding the legal definition of where you were when an injury occurred is the first step in determining how to recover compensation.

Amusement Parks

If you have a family member who was recently injured at an amusement park, you might want to get them help by seeking compensation. But in order to file a personal injury claim, there are certain things that you need to know about where you were and what happened.

“Amusement park” is a loose term that can apply to several different things. But how is an amusement park actually defined? And what regulations apply to amusement parks as opposed to carnivals, theme parks, and other similar locations?

An amusement park is defined as a park that has many different types of attractions, such as games, rides, and events. One important characteristic of an amusement park is the fact that it is built for long lasting operation. This means that the rides are stationary and do not change frequently. An amusement park does not change location.

The fact that the amusement park’s rides are stationary and that the park does not move is what separates it from other locations with rides, such as festivals, fairs, and carnivals. Festivals, fairs, and carnivals tend to be temporary and have moveable rides, unlike the amusement park.

Another similar and common event is the theme park. A theme park could fall under the category of amusement park, since these parks tend to be stationary. The difference is that an amusement park is a random collection of rides and games, while a theme park’s events and rides center on one theme. For example, Disneyland is considered a theme park because all of the rides and games revolve around Disney. This park is even broken up into smaller themed "destination" parks, such as Epcot, Animal Kingdom, Universal Studios, etc.

Sometimes, it can be difficult to differentiate an amusement park from a theme park. The good news is that this does not really matter from a legal standpoint. There aren't any federal guidelines to distinguish these types of parks. However, amusement parks and theme parks differ from carnivals, fairs, and festivals to a greater extent. This is due to differences in ride type (fixed vs. moveable), regulations, and employment standards. For this reason, you should differentiate between a park and a fair or carnival if you are going to take legal action against a location. You can learn more about these other types of venues in this chapter.

Waterparks

Enjoying water rides can be a great way to spend a summer day with your family. Unfortunately, waterparks are not always safe. When this is the case, accidents can happen and injuries can occur. If your loved one who was injured at a waterpark, your family might want to seek compensation. One of the first steps in the compensation process is determine what happened and where. Your loved one may have been using a water ride, but this does not necessarily mean that they were at a waterpark.

Waterparks have different regulations than other, similar places, such as amusement parks or carnivals.

A waterpark is like an amusement park, but it is made up of water rides or water versions of rides. A waterpark might include rides such as:

- Flume rides
- Water slides
- Wave pools
- Lazy rivers
- Swimming pools
- Water playgrounds
- Artificial surfing

A waterpark might be one part of a larger amusement park, such as the waterpark section of Six Flags. Or, a waterpark can stand on its own, such as Wisconsin Dells in Wisconsin, which is one of the largest waterparks in the country.

In addition to waterparks, you may have heard of a water play area. Water play areas generally have some of the same features and rides as waterparks such as swimming areas, water slides, and more. But, water play areas are usually available in places like public swimming pools or hotels. These are smaller versions of waterparks that likely have small rides, less supervision, and less regulation than waterparks do.

Indoor waterparks have also become a popular option in North America and Europe since the 20th century. Indoor waterparks are a good option because they are not seasonal. They can be enjoyed even in cold weather, which is a good option for families looking for something to do on winter and spring breaks. Indoor waterparks and water park resorts have become a vacation destination for many families. Because of their size, they can also house large thrill rides. While this offers fun for older kids, it is important that these parks are regulated just as an outdoor waterpark would be.

Fairs

Many families go to local fairs, especially in the summer months. While fairs can be a lot of fun, they can also be dangerous. If your child was injured at a fair, you might want to seek help by filing a personal injury claim. But before you do this, you need to make sure that you were indeed attending a fair, and which type of fair it was. Fairs, festivals, carnivals, and amusement parks can be difficult to distinguish between, so this information can be helpful.

A fair, also known as a "funfair", is defined as an entertainment activity or commercial activity that people gather to participate in. It is the characteristic of most fairs that they are temporary events that occur on a schedule. For example, a fair might occur on the same day once a year, or there might be a schedule that the fair will run for a few weeks during the summer. Common events that might take place at a fair include games, rides, food, music, etc.

There are many different types of fairs that might take place in different locations. Generally, fairs are meant to mobilize a community, and the size of that community might vary. For example, there is the street fair, which will celebrate a neighborhood. Because it is neighborhood oriented, the street fair will likely take place on the main street of the neighborhood.

Large cities oftentimes have street fairs in different neighborhoods every week throughout the summer months. This is the case in places like New York and Chicago. Smaller cities and towns also have fairs, although they tend to have less than large cities do.

Then there is the county fair. County fairs generally celebrate the agriculture, animals, food, technology, and recreation of a specific county. The theme of county fairs is still local to that county.

You might also attend a state fair, which is a larger version of a street or county fair. State fairs are usually an annual recreational and competitive gathering of a state. State fairs might include exhibitions that have won at a county fair. In many cases, a state fair is held during late summer or early fall.

Popular state fairs in the United States are the Minnesota State Fair, the Wisconsin State Fair, and The Big E, which takes place in New England. Even though state fairs started as local events, millions of people attend these fairs every year. While this is impressive, it can also make state fairs difficult to organize and regulate. It is important that you look out for your family's safety if you are attending a state fair.

Many fairs, especially larger fairs such as county and state fairs, contain carnival rides. You can learn more about carnivals and carnival rides in this chapter.

Festivals

Unfortunately, family fun at events such as festivals can turn sour if there is an accident. If your family was attending a festival and someone got hurt, you will want to get them help as soon as possible. The first step in seeking help is making sure that your loved one is ok. Take them to see a medical professional so that they can receive proper treatment. In addition, your family might seek legal restitution against the festival organizers or employees. In order to do this, you need to make sure that you were actually attending a festival and not some other event. Here, I will define the festival so that you can determine if your family was indeed attending a festival, and how to proceed.

A festival can actually be characterized as a type of fair. Like a fair, a festival is a community event in which members of the community gather to celebrate a common interest, such as religion, culture, food, etc. Oftentimes, festivals are temporary events. They might last for one day, a weekend, or a few weeks. Regardless of the time period, after a short period of time, the festival will end. It might be resumed annually, depending on the festival itself.

Festivals oftentimes incorporate food, music, local products, moveable rides, games, and more. In this way, festivals are similar to fairs. In fact, many people consider festivals and fairs to fall under the same category. However, there are specific types of festivals that can differ from fairs.

Church festivals are one very popular type of festival that takes place in many communities. Church festivals oftentimes take place in the summer months or early fall. Alternatively, church festivals can happen at any point in the year, related to significant religious events or being used as fundraisers.

Church festivals oftentimes incorporate food, music, games, and rides. If an injury occurs at a festival because of a moveable ride, you could deal with the ride company to sort out compensation. You do not need to sue the church in order to receive compensation.

Another common type of festival is a school festival. Oftentimes, school festivals are used to create a tight-knit community between students, parents, and school staff members. Festivals are also a good time to fundraise for the school and keep the community involved in school events. School events oftentimes include games, moveable rides, and food. Once again, if an injury occurs at a school festival, you could contact the outside vendors for compensation instead of suing the school.

Carnival

Chances are that you and your family members have been to a traveling carnival near your home, especially in the summer months when these carnivals are popular. Carnivals are different from amusement parks and other events with rides and games in a few ways. Understanding what a carnival is and how it differs from similar attractions is important in the event of an injury.

A carnival is most commonly considered a traveling type of fair. Carnivals are commonly made up of attractions such as:

- Games of skill

- Games of chance
- Merchandise vendors
- Thrill acts
- Food vendors
- Moveable amusement rides
- Animal acts

Not all carnivals will contain all of these attractions, but will likely contain some of them. Traveling carnivals are also characterized by the fact that they are not set up in a permanent location. They travel from town to town or state to state and set up for short periods of time.

Unlike fairs and festivals, carnivals are generally not tied to a community event or a religious event. Instead, they are put on by companies that travel from place to place. However, a traveling carnival might be hired by a fair or festival to provide amusement rides at their event. This is why sometimes you see carnival rides at fairs or festivals. Traveling carnivals oftentimes have contracts with local governments so that they can participate in large fairs, such as county or state fairs, as well as smaller events, such as church festivals or school festivals.

Common rides at traveling carnivals need to be small enough to put up and take down regularly over the course of the carnival season. Oftentimes, traveling carnivals bring rides such as carousels, mini railways, bounce houses, mini roller coasters, Ferris wheels, and tilting rides with them. Some thrill rides are also included in traveling carnivals, such as roller coasters and rides with drops. However, because these rides are not permanent, they can't get too big.

At fairs, festivals, or independent carnivals, injuries that occur on rides are the fault of the carnival company. The carnival is responsible for the rides. It is their job to make sure that the rides are set up properly, maintained well, and operated properly. Therefore, if an injury occurs related to a ride, you should contact the ride operators or carnival owner for compensation.

Parks and Playgrounds

Entertainment areas for children can vary greatly. For example, an outing to an amusement park is a lot different than a day spent at the local playground or park. But regardless of the venue, injuries can occur. If your child was injured on a playground or in a park, you want to get them help. The first step in doing this is understanding how parks and playgrounds are defined.

A playground, sometimes called a play area or a playpark, is a space that is specifically designed to accommodate child play. Many playgrounds typically exist outdoors, but there are also indoor playgrounds and play places. Even though playgrounds are designed for children, some children under or above a certain age may be excluded. This happens for the safety of all people using the playground. For example, some children may be too small to safely use equipment, or they may be too young to understand how to use it. Alternatively, older children may be too large for some equipment, and could break the equipment or injure themselves while trying to use it.

Modern playgrounds include a lot of different recreational equipment. Common recreational equipment on playgrounds includes:

- Swing sets
- Seesaws
- Jungle gyms
- Slides
- Sandboxes
- Tire swings
- Monkey bars
- Chin up bars
- Playhouses
- Mazes

Playgrounds also oftentimes offer spaces to play sports, such as basketball courts, tennis courts, soccer fields, baseball diamonds, and more.

A park is an area specifically set aside for recreation, enjoyment, and/or the preservation of animal life. Unlike playgrounds, parks are designed for use by people of all ages. Common features of parks include:

- Open fields for picnics, walking, or playing sports
- Biking and/or hiking trails
- Fountains
- Monuments
- Barbecue grills
- Picnic tables
- Areas for dogs to run off leash
- Bodies of water, such as ponds and lakes
- Space to play sports
- Small playgrounds
- Gardens
- Pools
- Skateparks

Parks can have playgrounds within them, but the larger area may be defined as a park.

At an amusement park or a waterpark, it might be clear to you who caused an accident. For example, an accident might occur because someone operated a ride incorrectly. Or, you might want to sue the park owner because they did not properly maintain their rides. However, parks and playgrounds rarely have people in charge of operating equipment. That is the responsibility of the people using the equipment. As a result, it can be difficult to determine who is responsible for an injury.

If an injury occurred because the equipment is not properly maintained, you can contact the Department of Parks and Recreation to determine who is responsible. However, if your child was injured due to their own negligence, they are responsible for any subsequent injuries. For example, if your child used the equipment in an improper way and was injured as a result, the injury could be their fault. Park and playground injuries can be tricky to figure out. If you need help with this, you can contact our office.

Regulations

It can be useful to understand the amusement park regulations in each state, so that you know how to keep your family safe no matter what state you are in. 44 out the 50 states have government regulation of amusement parks, which you can use as guidelines if you are trying to determine the source of an accident.

Some of the regulations of amusement parks include that all accidents must be reported within four hours. Injuries that must be reported are any that create risk of death, disfigurement, impairment of health, or loss of the function of an organ. Another regulation is that signs and first aid stations must be appropriately placed in the park.

Lastly, there must be a lifeguard who is over the age of 18 present at all times that a waterpark is functioning.

These regulations, along with others, prevent amusement park owners and staff from not getting rides inspected, not keeping the park clean enough, not warning park visitors of potential hazards, or taking short cuts with safety personnel. On the other hand, it is up to amusement park visitors to abide by the rules set forth by the parks that they are visiting. On any amusement park website, you can find the safety and conduct rules.

The regulation or oversight on amusement parks is inconsistent across the United States. There is no federal agency or laws that are in place to oversee the parks and rides and the federal government gives each state discretion on regulating its parks. Some states may have government oversight, partial government oversight, regulations only on inspections, or no regulation agencies. Below is a list of all 50 states and their regulation agencies. You can refer to these agencies for more information on regulations and what steps to take if an accident does occur.

- Alabama: No regulation agency
- Alaska: Department of Labor
- Arizona: No regulation agency
- Arkansas: Department of Labor

- California: Division of Occupational Safety and Health
- Colorado: Division of Oil and Public Safety
- Connecticut: Department of Consumer Protection
- Delaware: Office of State Fire Marshal
- Florida: Department of Agriculture
- Georgia: Office of Insurance and Safety Fire Commissioner
- Hawaii: Department of Labor and Industrial Relations
- Idaho: Division of Building Safety
- Illinois: Department of Labor
- Indiana: Department of Homeland Security
- Iowa: Workforce Development
- Kansas: Department of Labor
- Kentucky: Department of Agriculture
- Louisiana: State Fire Marshal
- Maine: Department of Public Safety
- Maryland: Department of Safety, Licensing, and Regulation
- Massachusetts: Department of Public Safety
- Michigan: Department of Licensing and Regulatory Affairs
- Minnesota: Department of Labor and Industry
- Mississippi: No regulation agency

- Missouri: Division of Fire Safety
- Montana: No regulation agency
- Nebraska: Department of Labor and the Office of Safety
- Nevada: No regulation agency
- New Hampshire: Department of Safety
- New Jersey: Department of Community Affairs
- New Mexico: Regulation and Licensing Department
- New York: Department of Labor, except for New York City
- North Carolina: Department of Labor
- North Dakota: No regulation agency
- Ohio: Department of Agriculture
- Oklahoma: Department of Labor
- Oregon: Building Codes
- Pennsylvania: Department of Agriculture
- Rhode Island: Building Commission
- South Carolina: Department of Labor, Licensing, and Regulation
- South Dakota: No regulation agency
- Tennessee: Department of Labor and Workforce Development
- Texas: Department of Insurance
- Utah: No regulation agency

- Vermont: Corporations Division of the Secretary of State
- Virginia: County Governments
- Washington: Department of Labor and Industries
- West Virginia: Safety Section of the Division of Labor
- Wisconsin: Safety and Building Division of the Department of Commerce
- Wyoming: No regulation agency

Unlike amusement parks, there is a governing body for carnivals. The Consumer Product Safety Commission regulates the hazards of carnivals, and investigates accidents or reported injuries that occur across the United States except for amusement parks.

Parents should be knowledgeable about the regulations and the oversight of amusement and carnival rides. The more regulations of rides, inspections, investigations and reporting requirements of accidents, the more likely the state is to have safer parks and rides. If you and your family love to travel to different states for amusement parks or are planning a family vacation, check out this list so you can be aware of the regulations on rides in that state.

CHAPTER 2: POPULAR AMERICAN AMUSEMENT PARKS

Chances are that there is a local amusement park in your area that your family loves to take day trips to, especially in the summer months. But there are also large destination amusement parks throughout the United States that families take vacations to. If you have kids, they have probably asked you to take them to some of these parks before. You might even remember a special vacation that you took as a child to one or more of these amusement parks. In this chapter, I am going to discuss some of the most popular amusement parks in America. This information can help if you are considering taking your family to one or more of these locations. Knowing what rides and attractions are at these parks can help you plan for a safe visit.

Walt Disney Parks and Resorts

When talking about American amusement parks, the first thing that comes to mind is probably Disney theme parks. The corporation's flagship resorts are Disneyland Resort, located in California, and Walt Disney World, located in Florida. In addition, there are Disney resorts in Paris, Shanghai, Tokyo, and Hong Kong.

Millions of people visit Walt Disney Parks and Resorts each year. Families use these resorts as vacation destinations, and many families visit every year or every few years. Chances are you have been to one of these resorts at least once in your life.

Disneyland Resort was the first location to open in 1955. It is located in Anaheim, California and owned by the Walt Disney Company. The complex contains two theme parks (which are a form of amusement park), Disney California Adventure and Disneyland Park. Disney California Adventure contains subsections, some of which are based on various Disney movies. The subsections include:

- Cars Land
- A Bug's Life
- Paradise Pier
- Grizzly Peak
- Buena Vista Street

- Pacific Wharf
- Hollywood Land

Disneyland Park contains subsections such as:

- Tomorrowland
- Frontierland
- Mickey's Toontown
- Adventureland
- Main Street, U.S.A.
- New Orleans Square
- Critter Country
- Fantasyland

In addition, the complex has three hotels, and a complex for shopping, eating, and entertainment known as Downtown Disney. The park contains many attractions such as shows, opportunities to meet characters from Disney films, food, shopping, and rides. Some common rides at the park are:

- Pirates of the Caribbean
- Splash Mountain
- Big Thunder Mountain Railroad
- It's a Small World
- Disneyland Railroad
- Indiana Jones Adventure
- Mad Tea Party
- Jungle Cruise
- Monorail

- Matterhorn Bobsleds
- Dumbo the Flying Elephant

Rides vary greatly at Disneyland. There are slow rides appropriate for young children, and thrill rides for teenagers and adults. Make sure that your children meet the requirements before letting them go on a particular ride.

The Walt Disney World Resort, commonly known as Disney World, opened in Lake Buena Vista, Florida, in 1971. Within the park, there are several theme parks, including Magic Kingdom, Disney's Hollywood Studios, Epcot, and Disney's Animal Kingdom. There are also two waterparks, Disney's Blizzard Beach, and Disney's Typhoon Lagoon. The property also contains 34 hotels and resorts. Common rides at Disney World are:

- The Tower of Terror
- Space Mountain
- Rock 'N Roller Coaster
- Test Track
- Seven Dwarfs Mine Train
- Kali River Rapids
- The Barnstormer
- Walt Disney World Railroad
- Dumbo the Flying Elephant

Disney's Resorts and Parks have so many rides and attractions, you will find something for the whole family.

But because thousands of people visit these parks every day, it is important to make sure that they are safe and in working order, staff members are paying attention, and you are paying attention to your children.

Six Flags

Six Flags is an amusement park corporation with 11 locations throughout the United States. Each location contains amusement rides, and some also have waterparks within the amusement parks. The locations are as follows:

- Six Flags Great Escape in Lake George, New York
- Six Flags New England in Agawam, Massachusetts
- Six Flags Great Adventure and Hurricane Harbor in Jackson, New Jersey
- Six Flags America in Woodmore, Maryland
- Six Flags Over Georgia and White Water Atlanta in Austell, Georgia
- Six Flags Great America in Gurnee, Illinois
- Six Flags St. Louis in Eureka, Missouri
- Six Flags Over Texas and Hurricane Harbor in Arlington, Texas
- Six Flags Fiesta Texas in San Antonio, Texas

- Six Flags Magic Mountain and Hurricane Harbor in Valencia, California
- Six Flags Discovery Kingdom and Hurricane Harbor Concord in Vallejo, California

Popular rides at different Six Flags locations include:

- X-Flight
- Justice League: Battle for Metropolis
- Vertical Velocity
- Superman
- Batman: The Ride
- The Joker Free Fly Coaster
- Tatsu
- Goliath
- Lex Luthor: Drop of Doom
- X2
- Thunderbolt
- Catwoman's Whip
- Scream
- Kingda Ka
- El Toro
- Nitro
- Skull Mountain
- Bizarro
- Medusa
- Kong
- Titan

- Mr. Freeze Reverse Blast
- Runaway Mountain
- Runaway Mine Train
- Road Runner Express
- The Great American Scream Machine
- Mind Bender
- American Thunder

Many of these rides are thrill rides, and many are located at multiple Six Flags locations. Remember to make sure that your children meet the requirements before you allow them on rides. Staff members should also check to make sure that the rides are operating correctly and they are being used correctly by passengers.

Hersheypark

Hersheypark is a theme park located in Hershey, Pennsylvania. It is owned by the Hershey Entertainment and Resorts Company, with many rides and sections of the park dedicated to different types of Hershey candy.

Like at Disney's parks, Hersheypark has themed regions. These themed areas include Founder's Way, The Hollow, Kissing Tower Hill, Pioneer Frontier, Midway America, and the Boardwalk at Hersheypark. The park also contains a zoo, called ZooAmerica, and several pools.

Hersheypark also contains many different types of rides. They have roller coasters, such as the Comet, SooperDooperLooper, the Wildcat, and more. Rides are broken up into five categories - children's rides, mild thrill rides, moderate thrill rides, high thrill rides, and aggressive thrill rides.

SeaWorld Parks and Entertainment

SeaWorld Parks and Entertainment oversees many large amusement parks and waterparks throughout the United States. The amusement parks include:

- Busch Gardens Williamsburg
- Busch Gardens Tampa
- Discovery Cove
- Sesame Place
- SeaWorld San Diego
- SeaWorld Orlando
- SeaWorld San Antonio

This company's waterparks include:

- Water Country USA
- Adventure Island
- Aquatica by SeaWorld, San Diego
- Aquatica by SeaWorld, Orlando
- Aquatica by SeaWorld, San Antonio

SeaWorld Parks and Entertainment's amusement parks and waterparks have fun activities such as amusement rides and water rides, live entertainment and shows from world class performers, and the ability to enjoy and learn about all different types of animals and plants.

While these parks are designed to be family friendly, their large size means that they require a lot of maintenance. Maintenance can be overlooked, as can operation. Make sure that you watch your children carefully and monitor which rides they use at the parks.

CHAPTER 3: AMUSEMENT PARK RIDES

Amusement parks are home to a variety of rides. Each ride presents its own entertainment, but also its own challenges. In this chapter, I will discuss some of the most popular rides at amusement parks. Understanding these rides can also help you understand ways in which they could be dangerous for your children.

Before we get into the rides themselves, here are a few general issues with parks, carnivals, and waterparks that could lead to injury.

Poor setup can be a cause for injury, especially at carnivals and fairs that have moveable rides. Workers must take down and set up rides quickly, sometimes within 24 hours and in the dark. The combination of tired workers and setting up elaborate rides in the dark can be a recipe for mistakes. If carnival workers are not trained correctly, they may be responsible for setting up rides that they have not been fully trained to handle. Another issue is that many carnival and fair workers are underpaid, and therefore, not as motivated to be careful and avoid making mistakes.

Poor maintenance can also cause issues at parks and carnivals. This can include not getting proper inspections of rides or not taking proper care of rides and fairgrounds. If there is a small issue with a ride, but the operator does not think that it is a big deal, they may choose to overlook it instead of making the issue known and getting it inspected. Carnivals and fairs also have little regulation on inspections, and may attempt to set up and operate without getting the rides properly inspected. It is also the duty of the park or carnival to keep the grounds safe from dangers like glass on the floor, or a sharp piece poking out from a ride.

Lack of supervision can also lead to injuries. This refers to not enough staff, lifeguards, or safety personnel at each ride or at the park in general, or staff that is poorly trained. At amusement parks, if there is not enough staff, people who are not trained properly may be operating rides or there may not be enough people checking safety belts and height and weight requirements at rides.

At waterparks, not having enough lifeguards or safety personnel can be a safety issue, especially if the park is overcrowded and there are a lot of small children swimming. Not having enough eyes on kids and the water can allow for drowning accidents to be overlooked. Lastly, if not enough time is spent on training staff, they may make mistakes that could be prevented.

Height and weight requirements are important for waterpark rides and amusement park rides because the ride manufacturers take into account the forces exerted onto one's body during a ride. If a child is too light or small for a ride, the seat and safety features of the ride may not be equipped for someone that is smaller than the posted size. Manufacturers also take into account the maturity level that is needed to follow the safety guidelines of rides when creating restrictions. When ride operators and staff at parks do not enforce these guidelines, it can put riders at risk.

Though rare, injuries can occur because of ride accidents that are due to mechanical errors. So much goes into all the mechanics and little parts that make up a thrill ride. However, sometimes oversights happen, rides may be old and worn out, or rides may be rusty. Having parts that are old and can break or parts that can fall off and hit people can be very dangerous.

It is also important to understand that there are two basic classifications of rides - fixed and moveable rides.

Fixed rides, also referred to as fixed-site rides, are rides that are permanently built into the ground and are not meant to move. You will most often find fixed rides at theme parks and other amusement parks, waterparks, and on playgrounds.

These rides are built to remain at such parks or playgrounds, not to be moved around from place to place. Oftentimes, fixed rides are therefore large rides such as big roller coasters, large water slides, and more. Thrill rides and large rides tend to be fixed rides because they do not need to be put together and broken down constantly in order to move to different locations.

The term "fixed" does not mean that these rides are impossible to move. They may be taken down and discarded or moved to a different part of a park. The distinction between fixed and moveable rides is that fixed rides are not regularly taken down and put up at different locations, like the rides at carnivals or fairs oftentimes are.

Because fixed rides are designed to stay in one place at amusement parks or waterparks, they can be very large rides that can reach great heights. A few examples of fixed amusement park rides include:

- Large roller coasters
- Water slides and most other water rides
- Large pendulum rides

- Large Ferris wheels, such as the London Eye or the Ferris wheel at Navy Pier in Chicago
- Log flumes
- Bungee jumping rides
- Reverse bungee rides

Thrill rides tend to be fixed rides instead of moveable rides. This allows for faster speeds, longer rides, and higher rides than moveable rides can allow.

Most playground equipment is also considered fixed. A few common examples include:

- Seesaws
- Swing sets
- Jungle gyms
- Sandboxes
- Slides
- Playhouses

This equipment is stationary and stays at the site of the playground, instead of moving to other playgrounds.

A moveable ride is a ride that is meant to be moved from location to location. Oftentimes, carnivals, fairs, and festivals utilize moveable rides. They are set up for the duration of the event and then taken down and moved to the next event.

Because these rides need to be constantly put together and taken down, moveable rides tend to be smaller versions of fixed rides. If you want really big thrill rides, you will have to go to an amusement park where there are fixed rides. However, there are smaller, moveable versions of fixed rides, such as moveable roller coasters, Ferris wheels, pendulum rides, etc.

Common moveable rides at carnivals and similar events include:

- Carousels
- Scrambler rides
- Kiddie rides
- Small pendulum rides
- Bounce houses
- Fun houses
- Tilt-a-whirls
- Zipper rides
- Big slides
- Train rides

Because moveable rides are put together and taken down frequently, you need to be careful when using these rides. Moveable rides can be damaged during a move or can be set up incorrectly. These issues could result in dangerous accidents for those using the rides. To prevent these injuries, make sure the carnival or fair has rented rides from a reputable company. You can also talk to staff members to learn more about their process of moving, putting up, and checking rides. This can give you peace of mind as your family tries to enjoy a fun outing.

If your loved one has been injured in a moveable ride accident, you should consider a few questions to determine who is responsible for the issue. Ask yourself:

- Did the accident occur because a ride malfunctioned? Could this malfunction have been avoided?
- Did the accident occur because of operator negligence?
- When was the last time the ride was inspected?
- Did the ride comply with regulations outlined by CPSC and other pertinent organizations?
- Did your child contribute to the accident? Did they use the ride correctly? Did they meet the requirements to use the ride?

These questions and more can give you an idea of what happened and who is at fault.

Now that we've discussed some general issues that could lead to injury and general ride classifications, let's look at specific rides and the dangers that they can present to people who use them.

Roller Coasters

Roller coasters are one of the most popular rides at amusement parks, and they are probably one of the first rides you would think of when considering accidents at amusement parks. Roller coasters can be fixed, such as large coasters at amusement parks. Or, they can be moveable rides, such as smaller coasters at carnivals and fairs.

It is true that roller coasters can be dangerous for various reasons. Because of the extreme heights and speeds that roller coasters can reach, small errors can be compounded and lead to serious consequences.

One issue that a roller coaster might face is derailment. Roller coasters wheels are railed in on three sides, so they cannot become derailed like a train would. Instead, a few different things would need to occur for derailment to happen.

First, if the aligners on the track were not lined up with each other. For example, if one aligner was in the center of the track, and the next aligner was shifted to the right. Second, a piece of the rail could bend or break off, causing a gap in rail. Third, bolts in the railings or in the roller coaster cart itself could break or come off completely, forcing one cart to detach and lose control. Next, a wheel could come off the cart due to a faulty axel or another part. Last, if the entire cart were to become detached from the set of wheels, it could cause derailment. Because roller coasters are moving at such high forces and speeds, any little part that becomes loose or breaks, can cause serious, deadly accidents.

Roller coasters can result in accidents. Every year, injuries are reported due to issues with roller coasters. Roller coasters can be made safer with more state regulations on inspections, more effective surveillance and data on injuries, better engineering of rides, shorter ride lifespan, better safety training for employees and ride operators, and more warning signs of medical conditions. Currently, besides riders failing to abide by the rules, many roller coaster injuries result from maintenance neglect, worn-out or rusty rides, operator negligence, and not enough importance being put on this issue.

Some common injuries that can result from roller coasters are:

- Lacerations, bruises, broken bones, torn ligaments
- Concussions and other traumatic brain injuries
- Stroke and brain aneurysms
- Paralysis
- Amputation
- Deathly falls

The truth is that roller coaster accidents do not occur that often. Luckily, these injuries are few and far between. But, when they do occur, someone or something is usually at fault. Unfortunately, sometimes injury can be the result of the rider not following the rules. Other times, however, injury occurs at fault of the amusement park or its staff, and could have been prevented.

Other common causes of roller coaster injuries include:

- Faulty harnesses and latches
- Rusty or damaged parts
- Operator negligence (starting or stopping abruptly)
- Poorly trained staff
- Poor maintenance
- Derailment
- Infrequent or improper inspections
- Defects in design and manufacturing of the rides
- Not following height and weight requirements
- Damaged seats or cushioning

Before getting on a roller coaster or allowing your children to, follow some of these safety guidelines. First, watch the roller coaster go around a few times to make sure there are no obvious issues with the ride. Also, watch the ride operators to make sure they are fully alert and paying attention. You should also follow all of the height and weight limitations. No matter how close your children may be, do not let them go on if they do not reach the requirements. Make sure to check the harnesses, seat belts, safety straps, and latches for you and your children when you sit in your seats.

Next, take out all items from your pockets, take off jewelry, glasses, hats, or anything else that could fly off you, as well as tie back long hair. Do not extend arms and legs during the ride or attempt to jerk your body or stand up. Please make your children aware of these safety tips before they ride a roller coaster as well.

Bumper Cars

Bumper cars are another very common ride at amusement parks. You see them at amusement parks, carnivals, and fairs. One aspect of the ride that makes it so popular is the fact that most people can go on this ride. Young kids all the way up to adults can ride bumper cars and enjoy them, but they do propose dangers in some cases. Although most places with bumper cars have warning signs saying not to bump each other, that's kind of the point and people rarely follow this warning.

Common injuries that can occur from bumper cars include:

- Broken bones, especially wrists
- Back and neck injuries
- Whiplash
- Concussion and other traumatic brain injuries
- Stroke due to trauma to ligaments in the neck

What happens with bumper cars is that, when two cars collide, the driver that is heavier or the driver moving faster will have more force. The problem with this is that bumper cars have drivers of all different ages, sizes, and weights. When you have a young child operating a bumper car, this may cause them to get bumped and spin in all different directions, with a great amount of force.

Even with a seatbelt on, getting jerked and jolted constantly and from all different directions, can cause someone small, or big, to hit their legs, wrists, head, or face on parts of the car. The neck and its muscles are also more fragile in children, and therefore, can become victims of whiplash and concussion, due to their heads slamming back and forth. Mechanical issues with the cars can also occur, leading to injuries.

When you or your children ride on a bumper car, you are assuming the risk of minor injuries that can result from collisions or bumps. Colliding, bumping, and sudden change in direction carries with it the potential for minor injuries. You cannot take away this risk without eliminating the "bumper" from "bumper cars". Therefore, you and your children should follow a few safety tips before getting in bumper cars.

- Follow the guidelines on restrictions to age, height, and weight
- Keep all limbs inside the car

- Always secure the seat belt and other safety belts
- If there are children on the ride that are behaving aggressively, report it to the operator and the manager

Before riding on bumper cars, make sure your child is aware of these safety rules, in order to be as safe as possible. Also be mindful that peer pressure may make younger children feel that they have to go on bumper cars and other rides, even if they do not want to. Before going on rides, make sure your child knows that they do not have to ride if they do not wish to.

Bungee Jumping

Most people probably know the obvious dangers and risks associated with bungee jumping. When you sign up to do the bungee jumping ride at an amusement park, you also sign a waiver that you are assuming the risks and dangers that come with this activity. However, there may be some things that this waiver does not include. For example, if you fall out of your harness, because an employee was being negligent and not paying attention, that does not fall under the foreseeable risk that you agree to take.

At many amusement parks and waterparks, there are bungee jumping rides. They are brought to the top of a tower and then release themselves from a connector and free fall until they reach the end of the bungee and fly back and forth in the air.

Before you or your children go on a bungee jumping ride, be aware of some of the possible risks:

- Harness, safety straps, belts, or latches failing to work
- Bungee cords getting tangled
- A cord can snap
- Cords not secured properly
- Miscalculations leading to cords that are not strong enough, hitting something on the way down

Though very rare, these mistakes can happen and can be very serious or fatal. Unfortunately, some amusement parks that contain these bungee jumping rides do not have landing mats or anything below the jumper to soften the fall. This is why the staff that work bungee jumping rides are trained to take all safety measures and double check everything. Unfortunately, even when they take precautions, they can make mistakes.

Luckily, the risk of death from bungee jumping is about 1 in 500,000. However, non-fatal injuries can be much more common. One common non-fatal type of injury to be aware of is neck injury, due to straining the neck during the jump. Another injury is damage to the eyes, due to the rush of blood to the brain after drastic changes in air pressure. Lastly, compression fractures and herniated disks can occur in the spine due to the force at which the body springs back up from the cord.

Before taking the jump, make sure your children are aware of some safety measures they can take:

- Disclose height, weight, and health issues as accurately as possible before riding
- Watch a few jumps before going to make sure the staff and ride is running smoothly
- Take everything out of pockets, take off jackets and hats, and tie up long hair
- Look at the bungee cords to make sure they are not faded in color, have any small tears, or look worn out
- Before releasing the lever or jumping, make sure all latches and cords are secured
- After jumping, try to keep head, neck, back, and limbs in line with each other

Another important element that is worth mentioning is that if you or a loved one goes bungee jumping and experiences minor pain in the head, face, neck, or back, go to the doctor and get it checked out immediately. In some instances, bungee jumpers have suffered serious injury, but did not feel intense pain until the next day.

Next time you or your loved ones decide to consider bungee jumping, remember the safety precautions above and follow your intuition! If you do not feel safe or comfortable, it is probably best that you do not go. Sometimes feeling anxious or stressed can cause you to tense up and risk injury as well. If you or someone you know has suffered an injury or wrongful death due to bungee jumping, please contact us for assistance.

Carousel Injuries

Believe it or not, carousels are actually on the list of top 10 most dangerous amusement park rides according to injury and death reportings. A carousel is a ride that you sit on as it slowly circles around while playing music. Children love to go on carousels. The problem with this is that so many young children go on carousels, that when there are slight issues, it can leave many small children vulnerable to injury, especially when riding alone.

Obviously everyone has heard about a roller coaster accident, but you rarely hear about a carousel accident. Carousel accidents actually cause 21% of amusement parks injuries to children under 18, according to the National Electronic Injury Surveillance System.

Carousels are typically a ride geared toward younger, small children. Parents may not go on the ride with their children, or may have multiple children to keep an eye on at one time while on the ride, or may be sitting on a horse next to their child. This means, many times, if a child loses their balance, even with a parent standing right next to them, they could fall over on either side of the horse. The horses on carousels have little to no safety belt or bar that secures a child in place. If a child falls off the horse, they can fall below the horse and get hit on its descent. The child can fall right off the side of the ride, while in motion, or fall behind and hit another horse. All it takes is a loss of balance for a small child to get seriously injured on a carousel.

Besides children falling off the ride because of losing balance, children can also fall off the ride due to mechanical problems with the ride, like starting or stopping too fast. Another problem could occur with faulty parts falling off, ropes getting loose and tangled, and ride operators not paying attention and starting the ride too early. If a mechanical issue or operator negligence occurs, it is important to report it to the park staff immediately.

Some safety measures to take when riding a carousel are to never allow a child under five years old to ride unaccompanied by an adult. The adult riding with any child should always put their arm around the child, to be able to save the child from falling to either side. If you have multiple young children riding, find a bench or seat on the carousel that can fill multiple people. If you are worried about you child losing their balance, find a horse or seat with a lap bar or safety belt, and fasten it tightly. Before riding a carousel, check to make sure that the operator is fully alert and paying attention. If this is not the case, report it to a manager immediately.

Spinning Rides

Spinning rides like Gravitron, Tilt-a-Whirl, Enterprise, and Music Express are favorite rides that can appeal to all ages. Some people hate these types of rides. These people often feel dizzy, nauseous, and completely sick after getting off a spinning ride. Others love the disorienting feeling and find these rides entertaining. Whether you love them or hating, you might wonder: how safe are these rides?

The Rotor or Gravitron ride is a circular chamber that spins around as the floor lowers, causing riders to stick to the wall because of friction and centrifugal force. The scary part about these rides is that they pin riders against a wall with a force that is three times the force of gravity. Rapid spinning and extreme forces of gravity can cause blood in the heart to pump faster to get blood to the brain. This ride may not be suitable for people that suffer from certain medical conditions.

The most common accidents that can occur are riders hitting against something or someone during the ride, getting pinched, falling down as spinning subsides, body pain from extreme forces, electric shock, seizures, and equipment failure. Other common occurrences include dizziness, nausea, and vision or hearing problems. These injuries usually occur because of a preexisting condition that a rider had such as a weak heart, asthma, or a neurological condition. Be cautious about riding these types of rides at amusement parks or carnivals if you have a medical condition, especially if these rides lack warning signs.

The Tilt-a-Whirl is a ride that spins carts on a platform, while going over small inclines, causing the carts to spin at all different speeds. This ride can spin at all different speeds and directions, making it unpredictable. Usually the Tilt-a-Whirl has very minimal safety restraints other than a bar that goes in front of the riders. This can cause riders to bump and crash into the sides of the ride and each other as the ride spins in all directions. The Tilt-a-Whirl should be ridden with caution if you suffer from a medical condition or get nauseous easily.

There have been reported incidents of passengers being thrown from their spinning cart and mechanical errors that cause the carts to crash into one another. When allowing young children to use this ride, be sure an adult is riding with them and making sure that they are properly restrained and will not crash into things as the ride operates.

The Enterprise is a ride that looks like a fast Ferris wheel from a distance, but the carts actually go upside down instead of staying right side up. These rides usually do not have seatbelts and only have a metal bar that comes down and is the same for all sizes. This lack of restraint can mean that small riders can rise up during the incline and hit their head on the top or fall forward coming down. The fast motion of the ride and strong force of gravity can lead to nauseousness, dizziness, loss of consciousness, and even brain hemorrhaging. Like other rides with strong gravity forces, they should be ridden with caution if you have medical conditions.

In the past few years, the Fireball ride has made the headlines on a few occasions. At the Ohio State Fair, there was an accident caused by a malfunction because of corroded pieces on the ride. Similarly, an accident at the Santa Cruz Boardwalk lead to a death and the ride was closed due to corrosion on the supportive beams of the ride. These accidents have called into question the safety of traveling rides like the Fireball that are especially dangerous, and may have a lack of supervision and enforcement of proper inspections. Witnesses to one of the accidents said that before the accident, they noticed a large crack on the ride. Before going on a ride like the Fireball, check the outside and report any issues that may stand out like rusty parts or cracks.

The Music Express is a ride that has connected carts that spin around in a circle forwards and backwards and over hills. Last year, in 2017, a girl was thrown from her spinning cart and broke her nose. When other riders and those on the sidelines saw what had happened, they screamed for the ride to stop, but the music was so loud that the operator could not hear them. Other safety concerns regarding the Music Express have been that riders can get pinned against the sides of their cart or collide within the vehicle, causing injuries.

Ferris Wheels

Luckily, Ferris wheels are fairly safe rides, especially when compared to other carnival rides. Ferris wheels are pretty laid back, there are no sudden drops, spinning, fast speeds, or crashing involved, but one major concern is the height and lack of restraint. Although Ferris wheels may not pose as much danger for small injuries, the types of accidents from this ride are usually falls, and can be very serious.

A majority of Ferris wheel accidents and falls result from riders not following rules and restrictions. Falls can occur when riders stand up from their seat in the gondola, attempt to exit before the ride stops, or swing the ride back and forth too forcefully. Unfortunately, many Ferris wheel falls have also been a result of operator mistakes and mechanical errors.

Regardless of who is at fault, parents should be cautious when letting young children, who may be less susceptible to following rules, ride without an adult. Many Ferris wheel falls have resulted from mistakes when young children ride alone. In one case, a young boy fell from the top of a Ferris wheel because it had stopped to let people off at the bottom and he got scared. When the young boy got scared, he panicked and tried to get out and fell. Other times, young children think it is funny to play around and forcefully push their gondola back and forth, resulting in someone falling out. If your children want to ride the Ferris wheel, make sure that they meet the height and weight requirements, and it is always best for an adult to ride with them.

Swing Rides

Swing rides can be found at amusement parks and carnivals and consist of chairs that are suspended by chains and rotate. Swings usually rise up high and make the riders feel like they are flying in the air. Swing rides are one of the most common rides, found at almost every amusement park and carnival across the country. Sometimes swings can be low to the ground and rotate slowly, and then there are swing rides like the SkyScreamer at Six Flags that can reach 125 meters in height and go over 40 miles per hour. Some swing rides even tilt at nearly a 90 degree angle.

There are several factors that can cause accidents on swing rides:

- Height and weight restrictions not being enforced
- Ride operator negligence
- Mechanical error
- Poor maintenance or inspection

One risk of swing rides is that the safety bar and strap can be removed by the rider. Because swing rides at amusement parks and carnivals usually have minimal size requirements, young riders, who are riding in a chair by themselves may get scared and panic. Kids who may not understand the importance of safety regulations may attempt to remove the safety bar and strap as well. Attempting to get off the ride and out of the seat before it has fully stopped can pose a risk as well. If a child falls or gets knocked over by another swing while attempting to get off the ride, they can suffer injuries.

Before your child rides on a swing ride, make them aware of the safety rules. Reinforcing the rules of staying in the seat, not touching the safety restrictions, and not getting off the ride until they are told can help prevent a future injury. No matter how cautious you are or how well your child understands the rules, accidents can happen.

Kiddie Rides

A lot of parents have concerns about letting their toddlers and small children ride the kiddie rides by themselves because they are too big to ride with them. Though the park may make these rides small, slow, and low to the ground, it can be difficult for parents to put their trust in an amusement park or carnival worker and a moving ride. Toddlers and kids can be clumsy, they can get scared without their parent, and may not be able to follow rules or have the capability to understand the rules of the ride. So, is letting your child ride alone on the kiddie rides safe?

Carnivals and amusement parks have very minimal height and weight requirements for kiddie rides. These rides are mechanically designed to be safe for little kids and make sure that there are appropriate belts, bars, and safety precautions taken. Kiddie rides are designed specifically for small children to ride without their parents going along with them. This being said, toddlers can be unpredictable and sometimes rides allow kids who can barely walk and talk on their own to ride. So although kiddie rides are designed for kids to ride, the unpredictability of kids' behavior can create the risk of fall accidents.

State safety agency data has shown that one third of fall accidents on rides are on kiddie rides. And of these falls on kiddie rides, a majority of the victims are two and three year old toddlers. This may be because children of this age can get scared when they realize that they are being taken away from their parent or when the ride moves, their parent is not in sight anymore. Young kids may panic and act impulsively out of fear. Toddlers are not always the best listeners and may try to undo their safety belt, unlatch safety bars, or stick their arms and legs outside of the ride while it is moving.

Some controversy in recent years has revolved around parents who try and cheat the height requirements for rides. If a parent knows that the height requirement is an inch or two taller than their child, they might convince the park employee to let them go on anyways, sneak the child on, or even put something under their shoes to make them appear taller. Never try and cheat the system that was specifically designed by the ride manufacturers for safety. Manufacturers set these requirements by accounting for safety that can protect kids of a certain size.

This being said, accidents can still occur on rides, even when a child meets the minimum requirements. Each parent knows their child's capabilities and maturity level. If your child meets the minimum size requirements, but you don't believe that they can follow the safety rules, it might be best to choose a different ride.

There are a few ways to take extra precaution if your child is riding on kiddie rides by explaining to them how they are to sit and behave on the rides. Explain to your child that they need to sit and remain in their seat the entire time. Make sure they know that you will be watching the entire time, and are not going anywhere. Set rules like their hands must be holding onto the ride, not lean over or out of the ride, and keep their feet on the floor. Remember that you know your child better than anyone and if a ride looks as though it may be too fast or too scary for your child, they should be accompanied by an adult.

Pendulum Rides

Pendulum rides are rides that have a fixed center on one end and a gondola or cart on the other end. As the ride takes off, the gondola swings back and forth, and sometimes all the way around in a circle. During a pendulum ride, the body is exposed to a certain amount of force due to the acceleration.

Though the body can handle small amounts and durations of this force, it could pose threats to those who are suffering from medical conditions or even minor stress on the body.

Some of the conditions that may make pendulum rides dangerous for riders are:

- Hyperventilation: If a person gets scared and starts panicking, the body may start to cope with this stress with short breathing. Hyperventilation can cause a lack of oxygen to the brain and can actually reduce the body's ability to cope with the force of the ride.
- Colds or infections: Someone who is suffering from a cold or infection may be more vulnerable to the impacts of force on the body, especially if they have a fever or are dehydrated.
- Heat: Heat stroke can cause the temperature inside the body to rise and increase dehydration,

which can compromise the body's ability to handle the effects of force from a ride.

If your child is suffering from a concussion, medical condition, or one of the conditions listed above, they should not go on thrill rides like a pendulum ride. Be cautious about children riding on these rides because they are more vulnerable to the effects of force from acceleration. If your child is scared or anxious about going on one of these rides, reassure them that they do not need to go on if they do not feel comfortable. Feeling anxious about riding can increase the chance of falls and other accidents.

Zip Lining

Both amusement parks and waterparks have zip lining. This is a ride where a rider is wearing a harness and travels from a high point gradually down to the ground. Some zip lines go through trees, some go over the park, and others go over water.

Many waterparks and amusement parks have several zip lines which require the rider to let go and drop into the water. The park also has others that start up at the top of cliffs and lead the rider into water.

Any ride that involves a rider hanging from a rope and a harness and going fast can lead to some risks of injury.

This risk is even greater when a zip line leads a rider into water, or a rider must let go and drop into the water. Letting go of a moving zipline into water, no matter what speed, can be dangerous because a rider can land in a harmful position.

If someone is moving while falling into water, there is a possibility that the rider will flip and land on their head or neck, or pull their back, or dislocate a shoulder. Even worse, if this rider falls on top of another swimmer in the water, both can get serious injuries or drown.

Zip lines that require riders to be harnessed and land in water can be dangerous because riders may land with a lot of force, or may flip and hit their head. The water can also get in the face and mouth, and cause suffocation. The other fear is that a rider can get tangled up in the ropes, cords, or harness when they hit the water.

Because many zip lines are up high, and require knowledge of properly harnessing and attaching riders to the zip line, the staff should be well trained. Zip lines can be upwards of hundreds of feet in the air, and no matter if there is water at the bottom or not, if a rider falls from those heights, they can be seriously injured. Staff who operate the zip lines must reliably strap on harnesses, attached the harness to the proper cords, and make sure that the timing is right and riders will not collide with each other.

- Some injuries that could result from zip lining are:
- Lacerations, bruising
- Rope burns
- Broken bones
- Concussion or other traumatic brain injury
- Strangulation
- Water inhalation
- Drowning
- Death

Though zip lining accidents are thankfully few and far between, it is important to be aware of the dangers and the possible injuries that can be caused when people make mistakes. Sometimes injuries can happen due to the fault of a rider breaking the rules, though often when this occurs, the rider may not have understood what the rules were.

CHAPTER 4:
AMUSEMENT PARK INJURIES

Unfortunately, injuries can occur at amusement parks. As mentioned in the previous chapter, there are many ways that an amusement park ride can malfunction and cause an accident. Although I touched on some injuries related to specific rides in the last chapter, this chapter will focus on common injuries that a person might sustain on multiple rides at an amusement park. You can learn more about common injuries in this chapter.

Whiplash

Whiplash is the sudden acceleration to deceleration force that moves the head and neck in a back and forth motion. This injury can result from rides that spin, like the tilt-a-whirl, on roller coasters that make quick turns, and any other ride that speeds up or stops suddenly. Roller coasters without a headrest behind the seat can be even worse, if whiplash were to occur, because there would be nothing to stop the head from being forced backwards.

Whiplash can be very minor or can lead to severe issues. The symptoms associated with whiplash are:

- Neck pain, neck stiffness
- Headache
- Back pain, shoulder pain
- Dizziness
- Nauseousness
- Jaw pain
- Arm pain
- Eye problems
- Ear pain

Usually whiplash symptoms only last a few days or weeks and go away on their own. It is best to seek medical attention if the pain is severe or effecting your child's daily functioning. Heat and ice is suggested for reducing pain, as well as an anti-inflammatory medication.

Whiplash can also lead to something called whiplash associated disorder that can have symptoms like insomnia or other sleep disorders, anxiety, depression, stress, and dependency on drugs. Whiplash can also vary in degrees of seriousness, because it can damage the bones, soft tissue, or both. Severe cases of whiplash or whiplash associated disorder may need to be treated with prescription medication, massage therapy, and physical therapy.

Whiplash is a common injury from roller coasters because the fast movements, starting, and stopping can easily cause the neck to be thrown forward or backward. Be careful of rides that do not have a back seat that extends up to support a person's head. Also, roller coasters that have over-the-shoulder straps and head support are generally better at preventing whiplash from occurring.

The risks of whiplash on roller coasters can be increased when ride operators do not enforce size requirement on the ride, when the seating or headrest of the ride is damaged, or if the safety belts and straps are too loose.

In order to help decrease your child's risk of getting whiplash on roller coasters or other amusement rides, check to make sure their seat and headrest are not damaged before sitting in the seat. Also, fasten their safety belts securely and tightly, so there is not excess room and let a staff member know if you feel the safety belt is not tight enough. Lastly, be sure to follow all posted height and weight requirements, even if the staff are not enforcing them. If your child is too short or too tall, the seating and headrest may not be adequately safe for their size.

Concussion and Head Injury

A concussion is a traumatic brain injury that is caused by hitting your head, or your head being forcefully shaken. Concussions can occur on amusement rides because of the abrupt stops, objects falling and hitting the head, or getting ejected or falling off of a ride. Concussions can also occur from the sharp turns many rides have, because this type of brain injury can easily occur from the head shaking from the force of a roller coaster. In some cases, a person might suffer from both whiplash and a concussion, due to having their head and neck shaken by a ride.

Roller coasters have also been known to cause another brain injury called subdural hematoma, which occurs when the blood vessels burst open. This condition can cause headaches, and must be treated medically with surgery. Another issue that may occur is decreased oxygen flow to the brain, causing loss of consciousness. This can occur when the G-force of the roller coaster is too great, because it can cause a loss of oxygen flow to the brain.

After a day at the amusement park, if you or your child is feeling sick or their head hurts, they may be suffering from a concussion or another type of head injury. Here are some of the symptoms to look out for:

- Headache, pressure in the head
- Dizziness

- Nauseousness
- Confusion
- Loss of memory
- Throwing up
- Fatigue
- Slurred speech

Sometimes the symptoms from a concussion or brain injury do not appear until a day after or several days after the initial accident. If you or your child experiences these symptoms several days later, you should seek medical attention. Some symptoms that can be experienced after a concussion or brain injury may be:

- Sleeping problems
- Trouble concentrating
- Irritability
- Changes in eating
- Excessive crying in young children
- Appearing to be dazed or confused

Oftentimes, people with certain medical conditions like seizures or aneurysms should already be careful about going on roller coasters and other rides, however, traumatic brain injuries and subdural hematomas could potentially be more likely for people with these medical conditions. Often amusement parks do not place warning signs for these medical conditions in front of roller coasters and other fast rides.

Broken Bones

Broken bones can occur from three different things including trauma, a medical condition that makes the bones weak, or stress fractures that occur from overuse. Most likely, broken bones from amusement park rides are the result of trauma. Trauma can occur from falling, or any kind of extreme force exerted on a bone. When too much force is exerted on the bone, it can move out of place, break, crumble, or buckle. If you suspect that a loved one has broken a bone at an amusement park, watch out for these symptoms:

- Bruising and swelling
- Bleeding and open lacerations or wounds
- Deformity of a body part
- Pain and throbbing
- Inability to move the injured area

The most common broken bone injuries are arms, wrists, and legs. Some more serious fractures occur in the neck, back, and ribs. Broken bones at amusement parks are usually a result of a crash or fall of some sort, however, broken bones can also occur from rides stopping too quickly or putting too much force on a body part. For example, wrist fractures can be a common bumper car injury because when a bumper car crashes, often riders will put their arms out to stop themselves from jerking forward.

Broken bones can be the result of ride accidents or the rider being ejected from their cart. If a ride operator does not ensure the safety belts and bars are secure, a rider can fall out of their cart during the ride. Mechanical errors or poor inspections can cause the ride to break and parts to come loose and hit riders during the ride. In these cases, fractures may be more severe and life threatening. Lastly, faulty seats or headrests can cause fractures to the neck and back, leaving the rider severely injured and requiring extensive medical treatment.

Although a bone can naturally heal on its own, medical treatment is usually required in order to make sure that the bone heals correctly and the person does not lose any function. A doctor might help by making use of:

- X-rays
- Pain medication
- Reduction, putting the bone back in place
- Casts and braces
- Metal plates and screws
- Metal rods
- Steel pins
- Physical therapy
- Surgery

Lacerations

A laceration is a cut on the skin that is deep, and can be especially harmful on the head or face. Lacerations can occur at amusement parks and waterparks when the skin gets caught on something and tears or gets hit by something with blunt force. Sometimes lacerations can occur when the skin gets caught on sharp objects that stick up on seats or slides. Other times, lacerations can occur from falling objects hitting the head or body.

If you or your child suffers lacerations on an amusement park or waterpark ride, stop the bleeding by applying pressure to the area. If it is possible, try to raise the affected area above the heart, as to stop blood from rushing to the wound. Once the bleeding has subsided, clean the area with soap and water and apply antibiotic ointment. Put a clean bandage on the area, and try to stay out of the water for the rest of the day.

If the laceration is bleeding profusely and non stop, and cannot be stopped after applying pressure, call 911. Sometimes, deep lacerations need medical attention and need stitches to repair the skin tearing. If the laceration is on the head or face, you must seek medical attention as soon as possible. It is important to stay away from water or other activities that may worsen the cut. If a lacerations touches water, it could be infected by germs and bacteria.

Lacerations can be minor or very serious, even fatal. Serious lacerations are usually those that have been exposed to dirt or debris and face possible infection, are so deep that there is bone or tissue exposed, or those that cause significant loss of blood. Also, lacerations on the head and face may be paired with other medical emergencies like concussion or trauma to the brain, because of a blow to the head.

Lacerations may need medical attention such as stitches, staples, hair tying, or surgery, involving going under anesthesia. Lacerations are not always fixed with this medical attention, however. There may be complications like scarring, reopening, bleeding through, and infection. Wounds, especially deep wounds, can also have risk for getting a bacterial infections from dust, dirt, or debris getting inside, causing tetanus.

Even cuts and lacerations are injuries that should not be taken lightly. Deep laceration wounds can cause serious pain, infection, and lifelong scarring or deformity. Even after getting treated, laceration wounds can lead to expensive medical bills. If you or a loved one has been cut by an object or ride at an amusement park, waterpark, carnival, or fair, call us to speak with an attorney about what you can do.

CHAPTER 5: WATERPARK RIDES

Waterpark rides can be a lot of fun, especially in the hot summer months. However, you and your family should exercise caution when using these rides. Malfunctions and other issues can cause injury. In this chapter, I will discuss some of the common waterpark rides, as well as proper and improper use of them.

Lazy Rivers

Lazy rivers are supposed to be the relaxing ride at the amusement park or waterpark. The point of a lazy river is to lay inside of an inner tube and gently float along a pool stream. And while this is generally more relaxing and safer than a thrill ride, accidents can still happen. These "relaxing rides" are notoriously overcrowded with people of all sizes and ages bumping into one another, splashing every which way, and toppling over. Small children may panic when they cannot control their tube or float away from their parent, teenagers may be splashing and roughhousing, and adults may be laying back with their eyes shut for a relaxing time, not paying attention to what is going on around them. Lazy rivers are often a stream of water filled with chaos. Unfortunately, riders, especially young children, are vulnerable to the dangers of lazy rivers. These dangers include:

- Overcrowding, which leads to bumping and crashing tubes
- Splashing water, chlorine, and glare from the sun, which can reduce vision
- The water is often deeper than children's heads and therefore, there is risk of drowning
- Loud noises and overcrowding make it difficult for lifeguards and safety personnel to hear people who need assistance
- Slippery tubes make it easy for children to slip
- Changing currents, uneven water

Lazy rivers are deceiving and are often thought of as a nice option for parents with small, young children to enjoy, rather than going on huge water slides and rides. While the lazy river is a less intense option than other rides, parents still need to be aware of the dangers, so they can prepare and be safe when planning to go on this ride, especially with children.

These dangers mentioned above can cause some serious injuries which include:

- Scraping against the sides or bottom of the lazy river, causing lacerations and bruising
- Broken bones from falling underwater and getting stepped on
- Water inhalation
- Bacterial infections
- Brain damage due to lack of oxygen
- Drowning

Similar to other personal injury cases that are caused by park rides, those who ride are accepting the possibility of injury when deciding to ride. Though there is foreseeable risk, sometimes the risk is made greater due to the lack of safety that is provided by the waterpark.

If the waterpark fails to train their lifeguards and safety personnel adequately, does not maintain proper inspections, does not keep their water clean, or does not have enough staff, they may be liable for injuries that may occur. If you or someone you know has suffered an injury, the medical bills can be expensive and place a burden on you and your family.

Flume Rides

Flume rides are another one of those rides that can seem safe and harmless, but can cause serious injury. Flume rides are a blast for kids and adults of all ages. You wait in line, filled with anticipation, load four or five people into a log-shaped float, and fly down a steep hill, while getting your picture taken. This ride is a classic, and usually operates with no trouble at all. Just like other rides, however, when there is an error or mistake, fun can turn to trouble very quickly.

Some injuries that can occur from flume rides include:

- Lacerations and bruises
- Whiplash
- Back and neck injuries
- Broken bones
- Concussion and other traumatic brain injuries
- Stroke
- Heart attack
- Slip and falls in the area around flume rides from excess water on the ground

These injuries mentioned above can be a result of any number of things. First, the log flumes are designed to hold several people in a single file order. With this positioning, along with the steep, sloped drop, the riders can end up falling into the person in front of them during the drop or at the bottom.

Next, another issue arises with safety belts. Often these rides do not have safety belts or have minimal safety protection and riders can fall forward and out of the ride, the person in front can slide forward and underneath the front of the ride, and riders have even greater chance of knocking into each other.

Also, the weight distribution must have the smallest person in the front and biggest in the back, allowing the possibility of the smallest person receiving the greatest impact of the drop at the bottom and collisions.

Lastly, injuries such as whiplash and concussion are possible on flume rides. Whiplash is common due to the sudden, steep drop and quick twists and turns throughout the ride. Concussion and other traumatic injuries are common in collisions with other people or parts of the ride.

Some safety precautions that you can take to help your children be safer and more prepared include telling your children to:

- Familiarize themselves with where safety personnel are located along the ride
- Always fasten any safety belts and straps on the ride
- Sit with their back touching your seat

- Keep all limbs inside the ride
- Take all items out of their pockets and tie up long hair
- Hold onto the railing or keep hands and arms inside the ride
- Do not look backwards or make sudden movements

It is important to remember that these injuries are not very common, however, being aware that they are possible and how they happen can help you and your loved ones be more prepared for riding on a flume ride.

Water Slides

Whether you are at an amusement park, outdoor waterpark, or indoor waterpark, water slides are perfect for the entire family to cool off and have fun on a hot day. These days, parks have been constantly expanding their options of water slides to add to the excitement, keep people coming back, and appeal to all ages. The main types of water slides that you will find at a park are inner tube slides, body slides, tunnel slides, slides in the dark, and raft rides.

Inner tube slides require the riders to sit or lay on top of an inflatable inner tube that gets sent down a slide filled with water. Inner tubes usually go a lot faster than body slides.

The main danger of inner tube slides is that riders can fall off of the tube. Many times parents wrongly assume that inner tube slides are safer because the tubes float, however, this may not be the case. The inner tubes gliding on the water can go very fast and are very difficult to control. If a rider lets go of their tube, they can fall off and get smacked by water or another rider. Riders who are going down the slide too fast may slam into other riders and send them flying off their tube or into the barriers of the slide.

The major risks of body slides are colliding with others at the bottom of the slide, hitting the sides of the water slide, and falling off the slide. Because riders are not riding on top of inner tubes, they can more easily smack their body against the slide while riding. This can also cause more injury if the rider collides with another at the bottom of the slide. When a rider does not have the protection of an inner tube, impact with another person can cause much more severe injuries.

Getting pinched or caught on ridges of the slide is a possibility, as well as hair getting caught on cracks or parts of the slide. Water inhalation, drowning, and falling off the slide are some very serious injuries that can occur from body slides.

Tunnel slides can be dangerous because the rider is unable to see what is going on or where the end of the slide is when they are riding. Inexperienced riders may already have difficulty holding their breath while swimming and jumping into water. When a rider is going through a tunnel slide, they may not realize they are at the bottom, and accidentally breathe in water.

Another risk is that riders may hit their body or head against the sides or top of the slide while going down and get injured or knocked unconscious. Young riders may get anxious or scared while riding because they cannot see anything, and this may cause injuries when getting to the bottom.

Slides that are in the dark can have similar risks as tunnel slides, because it is very difficult to see anything, and young children may panic and not be able to hold their breath or land safely at the bottom of the slide. Many injuries that result from slides in the dark are because people panic and start to breathe heavily, stick their arms out to stop, or try and sit up or move and end up hitting their head or body on the slide.

Raft rides are water rides that slide down a stream of water, sometimes while bumping against the sides of the water and spinning. The rafts usually hold 2-8 people and have seatbelts. The main concerns of this ride is hitting your body against the sides of the ride, or falling out of the ride. When the raft hits the sides of the ride, it can send the raft spinning and bumping into things and if someone's body is hit by one of the sides, it can cause scrapes, lacerations, concussions, and broken bones.

Falling off of the raft can be very dangerous because that fallen rider can get separated from the raft and get stuck in the current, swept over by waves, or smacked into rocks, the sides, or another raft. There are usually not staff positioned all over the ride, and therefore, there are no eyes on riders at certain points during the ride. If someone were to fall overboard, there would most likely be no one to help that person get out of the water or back onto the raft.

Waterpark Cliff Jumping

One attraction that can make parents nervous is the cliff jump. Cliff jumps usually have a lifeguard available in case there is an issue with the jump. A staff member should also tell kids when they can jump to prevent too many people jumping at once. If a cliff jump doesn't take these precautions, accidents can happen.

The safety issues of the cliff jump start with the fact that children can jump off a slippery rock that is high in the air and slip or land wrong. Though jumpers are instructed to jump with a straight body and arms crossed, children do not always follow or understand instructions. Jumping from a height can lead to serious injuries to the legs, back, neck, arms, and head.

Another issue with cliff jumping is that landing in the water might also be part of the swimming zone for other park goers. This means that people may get in the way of the landing or the jumper may accidently jump too far and hit a swimmer at the bottom. Landing on another person after jumping from such a height can seriously injure the person jumping and the person they land on. Not only will the person that gets landed on be knocked underwater, but the hit can cause them to suffer injury or get knocked unconscious before even going under the water.

Slipping can also be a hazard with the cliff jump, since the jumpers are jumping from a wet rock. Jumpers are allowed to take a few steps before jumping or jump from a stand still, but either way they could slip before making the jump. If a jumper slips before they jump, they could hit the rock cliff on the way down, go down the wrong way or head first, or land in the wrong area of the water and hit someone. Hitting the rock cliff on the way down can cause minor injuries like cuts and bruises or major injuries like spinal injuries or traumatic brain injuries.

Other Areas to Watch

Certain areas of waterparks can be more dangerous for young children and adults who are playing at a waterpark. Areas that can pose more risk than others at waterparks are those that are wet, high up, or can injure someone if they fall. Here are some areas in an indoor or outdoor waterpark to be cautious of.

Areas of a pool or attraction in a waterpark that have platforms for jumping or diving should be approached with caution. Young children who are jumping in the water may underestimate jumping away from the surface or ledge. A child may hit the side of the ledge or pool, may jump on top of someone, or may slip while jumping.

Before allowing your children to jump, especially off high surfaces, check to make sure that the ledge is non-slip, and that they are looking to make sure no one is near them when jumping. Teenagers often like to show off to their friends and take risks. If you have teenagers, make sure they know not to dive into shallow areas or to do flips off the edge of a pool.

Splash pads are typically set up like a playground and have jungle gyms, shooting water, and small slides. The one major danger of splash pads is the slippery surfaces. When children are gripping and stepping on parts of the playground, it can be easy to lose traction or slip and fall.

The other issue is that shooting water can spray into young children's ears, eyes, and mouth. Because waterparks have water filled with cleaning agents, chlorine, and germs, it can be harmful if swallowed. Advise children not to drink or swallow the water that shoots out of the ground or other toys on the splash pad. Shooting water can also lead to bacteria and infections spreading, as well as pose a threat of drowning from water inhalation.

At many waterparks, there is a giant water bucket that fills up with water and dumps all over the playground, sometimes every 10-30 minutes. Children playing love to run over and stand right under it as a countdown goes off and then as the water drenches them. A lot of people underestimate the force of this giant water bucket.

These water buckets generally hold about 1,000 gallons of water and come crashing down directly overhead. Small children may not be able to handle the force of this falling water, when standing directly below it. The force can result in slipping and falling onto the platform or ground they are standing on, falling onto other people and knocking them over, or swallowing and inhaling water. Be cautious about small children standing right underneath or on top of a platform that they can fall off of when the water bucket dumps.

Jumping areas, diving boards, splash pads, and giant water buckets should be approached with some caution, especially with young children. Young kids may watch older children doing more advanced things at the waterpark and mimic their behavior without understanding how dangerous it is. Explain the rules of the waterpark to your children before playing, and someone should always be with young children, especially on these types of activities at waterparks.

CHAPTER 6: WATERPARK INJURIES

Just as with regular amusement park rides, injuries can occur with waterpark rides. Some of these injuries are preventable, while others are not. In addition, some of them may be the fault of the park goer, while others may be the fault of the ride operator, maintenance team, or park owner. In this chapter, you can learn more about common injuries that occur in waterparks.

Waterparks may not have huge, fast roller coasters to ride on, but injuries are actually more common at waterparks than amusement parks. The combination of water, slippery surfaces, and small children running around may not always be the safest. Of course, when there is water, drowning is always a frightening possibility. But, there are many other common injuries that occur at waterparks on a regular basis. You can learn about them in this chapter.

Slip and Fall Accidents

Waterparks are filled with slippery surfaces like splash pads, ride platforms, playgrounds, and staircases. Besides being slippery, waterparks are usually filled with hundreds of young children who are playing, running, jumping, and this can lead to slipping and falling accidents. According to Consumer Product Safety Commission, there are about 15,000 slip and fall accidents reported each year, which is about 40% of all amusement park injuries.

Slipping and falling can lead to a minor bump on the elbow or scrape on the knee, but sometimes, injuries can be much more serious. Slip and falls at waterparks can lead to serious injuries such as:

- Face injury
- Neck and back injury or fracture
- Bones fractures
- Spinal cord injuries
- Paralysis
- Traumatic brain injuries
- Drowning

There are some issues that may cause slipping and falling at waterparks, including slippery ground or stairs that do not have non-slip material on them, lack of cleaning, warped and damaged wood surfaces, and lack of restraints on inner tubes and water slides. The combination of slippery slides and tubes, fast speeds, and lack of restraints can increase the likelihood of falling off waterslides and onto the surface below.

With slip and fall injuries, it can be difficult to know who is really "at fault". Who is at fault depends on what the conditions were, the circumstances involved in the accident, and whether guests are warned of slippery surfaces. If your child slipped and fell at a waterpark, consider these questions to help determine if you have a case:

- Was there a caution sign warning park goers of a slippery surface?
- Was a slippery surface ignored by the staff for an unreasonable amount of time?
- Does the park use a waiver, and if so, does it say anything about slippery surfaces?

These factors and more could play a role in determining fault for a slip and fall accident.

Some ways to be more cautious at waterparks to prevent slip and fall injuries are:

- Abiding by all rules, regulations, and especially warning signs. Avoid the areas that have "danger" or "warning" signs posted
- Have an adult present with children when going from ride to ride and waiting in line, especially on stairs with them

- Reinforce the rules of not running or pushing
- Avoid areas that look slippery or unkept
- Look around and make sure that there are lifeguards and safety personnel that are alert

Bacteria and Germs

Thousands of people go in and out of the water at waterparks all summer long. With everyone sharing the same water, even with chlorine and other cleaning agents in the water, bacteria and microorganisms are floating in and around the park that your children can be exposed to. Some of these could be E. coli, Legionnaires' disease, cryptosporidium, and many others. These bacteria and microorganisms can be very serious and can lead to vomiting, seizures, or even death when they grow and spread. It is especially important that children do not swallow or drink the water because of these bacteria. These bacteria can spread from urine and fecal matter, so do not allow young children who are not potty trained yet to go in the water without a swim diaper.

Make sure you go over the rules of the waterpark before your children go in the water. To prevent these health hazards from occurring, take occasional breaks from the water and sun, young children should be taught to not swallow the water, and wash off the feet and body when out of the water and at the end of the day.

Recreational water illnesses (RWI) can affect the skin, ears, respiratory system, brain, or gastrointestinal system. They are found in water that is contaminated by germs or chemicals and they are contracted through germs from swallowing, inhaling, or contact with cuts. Water illnesses can also occur from chemicals in the water at waterparks, and can spread from germs in the water at waterparks.

RWI can include many different types of illnesses such as:

- Diarrhea
- Skin rash
- Respiratory infection
- Chemical burn of eyes and lungs

Other illnesses that can spread through towels and unclean waterpark facilities include head lice, MRSA, and pinworm. This being said, when you are at the waterpark, it is best not to allow your child in the water if they have had an upset stomach or diarrhea because that could spread to other children in the water. If you or your child has an open wound or laceration, it is best to avoid the waterpark or other recreational waters as to not contract germs and illnesses that could spread into a wound. Also, make sure that if your children are not potty trained, that they are wearing waterproof diapers into the water.

Waterparks can also be a huge source of fungal infections like athlete's foot. Athlete's foot and other viruses could cause foot warts. It is best to rinse feet thoroughly before and after playing in the waterpark. Another suggestion is to wear water shoes which could help to prevent slipping as well as prevent foot fungus from spreading. Some issues to watch out for include:

- Legionnaires' disease: Caused from the breathing in of small water droplets, like mist, which oftentimes you will see at waterparks. When the pumps that release the water mist are not properly cleaned and disinfected, the infected water droplets can get into the lungs and respiratory system. This can lead to pneumonia, which is a serious illness. It could even be fatal.
- Cryptosporidium: A parasite that spreads through human feces and can cause stomach pain, fever, nausea, vomiting, diarrhea, and weight loss. These symptoms usually appear days after the initial contact, so keeping an eye out for these symptoms after going to the waterpark can be helpful to not mistaking it for the flu.
- Hepatitis A: Usually spread through contamination of water with fecal matter. The

symptoms for Hepatitis A could include fever, liver pain, rash, fatigue, and yellowish skin. Be especially mindful of Hepatitis A and its symptoms if you or your child has a chronic liver illness, because it will be harder to fully recover from Hepatitis A with this type of illness.

These recreational water illnesses can be present in water that is not properly cleaned and maintained. If you see water in the park that is an odd color or looks cloudy, report it to a manager or staff member at the park. Remember to take safety and health precautions like wearing watershoes, putting young children in waterproof diapers, and taking showers right after the exposure to a waterpark.

Lacerations

A laceration is a cut on the skin that is deep, and can be especially harmful on the head or face. Lacerations can occur at amusement parks and waterparks when the skin gets caught on something and tears or gets hit by something with blunt force. Sometimes lacerations can occur when the skin gets caught on sharp objects that stick up on seats or slides. Other times, lacerations can occur from falling objects hitting the head or body.

Lacerations at waterparks can be especially harmful, because they can allow germs, chemicals, and bacteria from the water to enter a person's body. Refer to the information about lacerations in Chapter Four if you need to know more.

Drowning

The risk for drowning is a real, but a rarely talked about topic. Unfortunately, drowning does occur at waterparks, and these parks can pose risk to children, especially small, inexperienced swimmers.

Parents of course do their best to keep an eye on their children and make sure that they are safe when swimming and playing in water, however, drowning can occur within seconds. Children who are not strong swimmers should be wearing a flotation device at all times when playing in water or should be accompanied by an adult. Unfortunately, waterparks can be so crowded and have so much happening at one time, that lifeguards can make mistakes or not realize that a child may be drowning.

Even children who may be strong swimmers can get tired while swimming or can get swept underneath the water by a tide or other children. Kids are more likely to panic than adults when breathing in a little water or getting pushed underwater, and this can make them more vulnerable to drowning. Kids are also very active and curious. Kids can be playing and may accidently swim into a deeper part of the water or venture away from watching eyes. It is important that children play and swim together in pairs, so that no one is in the water alone.

Waterparks have some extra risk factors that can lead to drowning as opposed to parks, swimming pools, and amusement parks. It is best to understand these risk factors, so you can be prepared when you go to a waterpark to prevent tragedy from occurring. Here are some of the factors that may increase the risk of drowning.

- Overcrowding: Overcrowding is common at waterparks. Having too many people and children playing on slides, splash pads, and pools can mean that there are not enough lifeguards to watch over everyone, and can lead to mistakes, accidents, and oversights.
- Different rides, heights, activities: Waterparks are usually wide open spaces but have various pools, slides, and activities of different sizes and heights. Having a large space with lots of different rides to run around and play on can make it easy for parents to lose sight of their kids, or for their view to be blocked. This can

also allow for kids to go in separate directions and parents may not be able to keep track of their children playing on different things.

When going to the waterpark, be aware of these risks and take preventative measure such as the buddy system, flotation devices, and staying with your child in the water the entire time. No matter how careful you are, accidents can happen.

The number one fear of pretty much every parent at a pool or waterpark is their child drowning. However, many parents may not know that there is a risk of drowning even when a child is not in the water. This type of drowning is from water inhalation and can be known as “dry drowning” or “delayed drowning”. Dry drowning is a very serious condition and can lead to brain damage and death if left untreated. It is important for parents to know how this dry drowning can occur and the symptoms to look out for.

Dry drowning can occur when a small amount of water is inhaled and gets trapped in the lungs. When the water builds up in the lungs, a condition called pulmonary edema can develop. This water can be inhaled while swimming, going down a water slide, or from shooting water on splash pads. Water hoses and water shooters at splash pads can be dangerous for small children if the water shoots into their mouth. The end of water slides where children are launched into the water by surprise can also be dangerous if the child does not hold their breath or lands in water as they are breathing in.

Dry drowning can lead to death when left untreated. Unfortunately, people who inhale water can appear fine for days until they even develop symptoms, and this makes parents not even associate the water with the symptoms. The symptoms of dry drowning are trouble breathing, coughing, chest pain, fatigue, dizziness, and behavioral changes. The issue is that these symptoms can easily be mistaken for being sick with the cold or flu.

If your child experiences these symptoms after going to the waterpark, go to the emergency room immediately. Dry drowning is treatable with ventilation to remove water from the lungs. When you and your children are at the waterpark, keep a close eye on small children who may have difficulty swimming and holding their breath. If your child has a non-fatal drowning experience in the water, be especially careful to look out for these symptoms of dry drowning.

CHAPTER 7: CARNIVALS, FAIRS, FESTIVALS

Amusement parks and waterparks are not the only festive options for the summer months. Each state is also home to many festivals, traveling fairs, and carnivals. I already defined these venues in Chapter One, but this chapter discusses these places and potential hazards that go along with them in greater detail.

State regulation of traveling carnivals and fairs are non-existent in many states across the country. Only 17 states require state inspections of the fairs and rides. Most of New England, for example, only requires third-party inspections. Carnivals and fairs go up and come down all summer long and into the fall in each state. They also travel throughout the state. Many workers who are putting up the rides and taking them down work long hours and sometimes work in the summer heat and at night in the dark. Without having strict state inspections, and given the conditions that these workers work in, are these types of rides as safe as permanent rides at amusement parks?

There are some serious problems with many traveling carnivals and fairs. The workers who are taking down and assembling the rides are also the ones who are operating the rides for hours. Another issue is that carnivals do not make a huge profit margin. The amount of money that it takes to haul traveling rides, pay workers to assemble, take down, and operate rides, and pay all of the insurance fees, does not leave much of a profit for many carnival companies. Carnival workers do not make much money either, and these conditions may lead carnival companies and workers to cut corners with safety.

Carnival rides might seem flimsy, shaky, and look as though they might uproot and fall over. As far as the rides themselves, statistics show that more emergency visits result from amusement park rides as opposed to carnival rides. However, carnivals have a short season, compared to amusement parks, which could sway these statistics.

It is best to be cautious and aware of safety hazards at both amusement parks and carnivals or fairs. Both have workers who may be working long hours, and may be tired and dehydrated. Before you put yourself or your child on a ride of any kind, observe the operator, and the rules and regulations of the ride. If you notice a ride operator drifting off, chatting while working, or just not paying attention; report it to the park manager.

Also, make sure that your children are aware of the rules and follow them. If the ride rules say to not carry any objects onto the ride with you and keep all arms and legs inside, make sure your child follows these rules. If you do not think that your child can follow the rules of the ride, go with them or maybe choose a different activity to do at the park.

Haunted Houses

Haunted houses can be found at many fairs and carnivals and even at amusement parks. Haunted houses are one of the only times people actually pay to be terrified and feel in danger. But how far is too far in trying to scare people? Do injuries happen at haunted houses?

Haunted houses are usually dark tunnels or rooms with people dressed up in bloody, gory costumes popping out and letting out blood curdling screams. Sometimes, when people get injured in a haunted house, it can be almost impossible to even know because of the darkness, fake blood, and screams of terror that are already happening. Before you, your friends, and your family head to a haunted house, be aware of some of the injuries and accidents that could occur.

People usually walk or ride through haunted tunnels and houses in large groups of people. Some jump from terror, or try and run away from something popping out at them, or throw their arms up from being scared. Especially in the dark, it can be difficult to see others around you, especially small children. Trampling can occur when so many people are moving all over the place, and can be even worse when the screams of someone getting stepped on are being masked by the screams of the attraction.

Haunted houses usually have objects hanging and large props set up to set the eerie tone. With so many people jumping, running, and moving everywhere, props can fall into people or on top of people. This can become a serious accident if a small child gets hit by a falling prop that is much larger than them.

Scary objects that are usually used in haunted houses are chainsaws, knives, or other protrusions coming from the walls or props. With large groups of people going through a dark house, it can be easy to get cuts or bruises from bumping into these objects. Even if they are fake, they can still cause damage if ran into.

Many haunted attractions have fake smoke machines or fog machines. These machines let out fake smoke that has chemicals in it, and in an enclosed space that does not have enough ventilation, people can breathe it in and suffer from the fumes.

Sometimes the actors who are trying to scare people in haunted houses can jump out at people, or even grab them. There have been incidents where this is taken too far and someone actually falls and gets injured, or experiences a heart problem due to fear. A person also might experience anxiety symptoms such as heart beating too fast, difficulty breathing, or getting an anxiety attack.

If your child wants to go in a haunted house, it is a good idea to accompany them. Staying close to your child can help you distinguish between normal fear induced by the haunted house and a serious injury that needs to be addressed.

Inflatable Bounce Houses at Carnivals

Many states do not regulate inflatable amusement devices at carnivals and fairs, but some states regulate these devices through the Department of Consumer Protection. Part of the regulation on inflatable bounce houses at carnivals and fairs includes annual inspections as well as safety warning signs. Though bounce houses are regulated, there is still the chance that accidents will occur.

In 2016, the Consumer Product Safety Commission estimated over 20,000 injuries resulting from inflatable bounce houses, which is more than double the injuries from a decade ago. Some accidents that could lead to injuries in bounce houses are:

- Skin burns: Also known as friction burn, can occur when the skin rubs against the material on bounce houses, especially bounce house slides. When kids slide down slides, the vinyl material can cause a nasty red burn that can be very painful. The best way to avoid this is to be wearing long sweatpants and socks when playing in a bounce house, to avoid skin contact with the vinyl material.
- Bruises or broken bones: The most common fractures are to the legs, feet, hands, and arms. It is difficult for jumpers to maintain balance in the bounce house. Especially toddlers who have just learned to walk can easily trip and fall or bounce too high and not be able to land stable on their feet. Landing wrongly on the ankle and twisting it can lead to foot and ankle fractures and throwing the hands and arms behind or in front to stop a fall can lead to fractures.
- Knocked out teeth: The jumping and colliding of children in bounce houses along with the netting

can knock kids' teeth out. This is likely not a big issue for kids with only baby teeth, but if an adult tooth comes out, this can present a bigger issue that must be fixed by a dentist.

- Concussion: Concussion or other head injuries usually occur when two jumpers collide with each other or when a child loses control and lands on their head. Instructing your children not to intentionally try and bounce into other children and telling them to bounce in their own area, can help reduce the likelihood of collisions.
- Neck Injury: The neck and spine are very fragile, especially in children. Neck injuries can occur when landing the wrong way, coming down on the neck or head, or colliding with others. If an accident occurs, your child may have a hard time identify a neck injury for themselves, so keep an eye out for symptoms afterwards.

There have been several incidents where bounce houses have been lifted into the air and have traveled in the air and then fallen with children inside. This accident can occur when the bounce house is not anchored properly. If this happens, children can suffer all of the injuries above or even death from the fall. Before your children play on an inflatable bounce house at a carnival, make sure that you see the bounce house is anchored or tied down in some way. Instruct your children to not climb onto the side of the wall of the inflatable, to avoid it tipping over.

Being Safe at Fairs

Fairs both large and small are common summer attractions. Many state fairs, such as the Wisconsin State Fair, the Minnesota State Fair, and the Big E, attract millions of visitors during the few weeks that they run. Such large crowds can be a lot of fun, but they can also be dangerous. They can put pressure on staff members to move quickly and overlook safety regulations. They can also present challenges such as families getting separated. Here are some tips on staying safe while at a fair.

If you want a bite to eat, fairs have all types of food vendors with your classic carnival food and some unique treats, and there is also usually a section of the fair with local foods. Fairs havelivestock, horse shows, agriculture events, farm animals, and a circus. For entertainment there are parades, street performers, and concerts. Also, you can find a museum, shopping at all the state houses and vendors, and all different types of competitions. Lastly, there are all different types of carnival rides and games.

One thing to be careful about at large fairs is the food that you are buying at vendors and various places. The workers are in tight areas, cooking order after order without breaks, and are usually in the hot sun all day. Sometimes these conditions can lead to tiredness and mistakes. The fair food may be susceptible to cross-contamination, bugs landing on it, touching chemicals, or sitting out too long. Workers may also neglect to keep their hands and work station clean, leading to bacteria contaminating food.

Before purchasing food, make sure to:

- Look at the workstation where the food is being prepared to make sure it is clean
- Make sure to let the vendor know if you have a specific food allergy
- Do not let food that you bring with you or buy at the fair sit out for longer than two hours, especially on a hot day
- Before eating or touching food, make sure to wash your hands first, especially after touching the livestock

Another huge component of many state fairs is the farm animals, livestock, horse shows, and petting zoos. Before you or your children take part in visiting and touching the animals, take note of these tips:

- Wash your hands or use hand sanitizer immediately after touching or feeding the animals, to prevent harmful germs that could carry diseases

- Do not take any baby items like bottles, pacifiers, or strollers into livestock barns
- Supervise young children when petting and feeding animals
- Young children and senior citizens, especially with weak immune systems, should be cautious of animal exhibits and petting zoos

Another component of these fairs is the parades that take over the streets. Parades have huge moving vehicles, floats, loud music, street performers, crowds everywhere, and candy, beads, and objects being thrown. It is important that young children be held or supervised during parades. Children who are not supervised can be vulnerable to being trampled, losing their parents, hit by a moving vehicle, or hit by something being thrown.

In order to keep children safe during a parade, consider watching from a distance, so your children do not run out in front of floats to catch candy being thrown. Also, hold toddlers and small children, so they are not stepped on or knocked over by anyone. Dress children up in bright, identifiable clothing, so they can be found easily if you lose sight of them.

CHAPTER 8: PERSONAL INJURY

If your child has been injured at an amusement park, carnival, waterpark, or similar place, it is time to get them help. This chapter will explain some of the ways that you can protect your child and make sure that your family recovers from the injury.

One of the first things that you should do if your child is injured on a ride or at a park is to seek medical attention. If the injury is a laceration or small cut, locate a first aid kit on the premise and bandage the wound. If the wound is bleeding a lot, go to the hospital. For a head injury, it is better to be safe than sorry, and if there is possibility of concussion, it is best to seek a doctor. For a neck injury, the injured person should be kept still and not move, and call 911. If the injured person is not breathing, perform CPR and call emergency medical services immediately. If you or your loved one feels dizzy, nauseous, or out of it after going on a ride, it is best to seek medical attention as soon as possible.

After seeking medical attention, you should take some initial steps in the event that you want to file a personal injury claim. Even if you are not sure that you want to file a claim, or not sure if you have a case, it is easier to take certain steps right away, rather than wait until you make a final decision about a claim.

While you are still at the park, it is a good idea to take pictures of the area in which the injury occurred and the ride that caused the injury. Taking pictures of the ride may be helpful in the event that you seek legal assistance and need to prove unsafe conditions or an unsafe ride. Also, take down the name of the ride operator and any witnesses nearby who may have seen the injury occur. Take notes on exactly what happened and any other information that may be key to what happened during the injury.

Next, report the injury to the manager. If you believe that the injury occurred because the ride operator was not paying attention, report that worker. Also, let the manager know if the injury occured because of a ride malfunction. If you suspect that the injury was due to a ride malfunction or ride operator's negligence, report the incident to the authorities to make a police report.

Finally, document your child's injuries. This will be done by taking them to the doctor, as a doctor will provide a medical report that you can use as evidence. In addition, you can take photographs of your child's injuries throughout the healing process to help prove them.

After you take these initial steps towards building a case, you should try to determine if you have a case. To do this, you need to determine who was at fault for the accident, and if you can prove fault in court.

Fault

Sometimes, accidents at waterparks and amusement parks just happen and no one is at fault. Other times, the riders do not follow the rules and regulations of the ride or park, making them liable for their own injuries. But in some cases, accidents are the fault of someone's negligence. At amusement parks and water parks, the manager, ride operators, and staff have a legal duty of care. This means that they must be properly trained, have enough staff to oversee all aspects of the park, have enough properly trained lifeguards and staff members on duty, post warning signs, enforce their rules and regulations, and maintain the park and inspections that are required. When the park does not maintain these standards of care, they may be at fault for accidents and injuries that occur.

Some causes for accidents that could be someone's fault include lack of training. Lack of training could include any of the staff at the park such as lifeguards, ride operators, ride staff, or managers. If someone is not properly trained for their job, they may make mistakes because they did not know what to do or what not to do.

Another cause for accidents is a lack of staff placed at a certain ride or location, or lack of staff on the premises of the park. Lack of staff is usually the fault of whoever makes the schedule for the park employees. Understaffed parks can lead to injuries. For example, if there is a lack of lifeguards at a waterpark, and there is no staff member at a water slide, this can allow young children to break the rules, or have unnecessary accidents because they were not monitored.

A lack of ride staff or operators could cause someone who is less experienced to be operating the ride before they are ready. Lack of ride staff could also mean rushing to check if kids are fastened into rides or if the rider in front of them has left the bottom of the water slide.

Sometimes staff members make mistakes, no matter how well trained or experienced. This issue is especially problematic in overcrowded areas or on busy days. With so much movement and people everywhere, children could be overlooked, and this could lead to injuries. In addition, staff members can make mistakes when operating rides.

Another cause of an accident is improper warning signs or height and weight enforcement. If the waterpark is lacking signs that warn visitors against risks and hazards, this can cause safety issues and riders not having the knowledge they need to decide whether they should go on a ride or not. Also, failing to enforce height and weight requirements of rides can allow for children who are too big or small to go on a ride and get injured.

Lastly, accidents can be caused by the lack of proper ride or park inspection or failure to maintain the rides or park. It is the responsibility of the park owner to make sure that the rides, slides, and park are properly inspected. If a problem with a ride is overlooked, and not inspected, it could put riders in danger. Similarly, owners must make sure that the rides, locker rooms, and entire premise of the park are maintained properly. Not maintaining the rides or the park could mean broken items, loose parts on a ride, broken glass, and dirty locker rooms or facilities.

Part of determining who is at fault for an accident is determining if there was a duty of care and if that duty of care was breached. If an employee had a duty of care towards your child and breached that duty, they could be held liable for your child's injuries. Duty of care is a legal responsibility to take care of someone and ensure their safety. Amusement park workers have a duty of care to make sure that park goers do not have any foreseeable accidents.

Amusement park workers have one major responsibility, which is to make sure guests at the park are safe. If a worker fails to act with duty of care, or acts in a way that a reasonable worker would not act in the same situation, the worker or the employers of the park may be liable.

When a park hires workers, they usually make sure that they have these understandings and qualifications, know the rules of the park, and are capable of the duty of care that is expected in order to keep guests safe and not have the park be liable. Sometimes mistakes can occur either because of an unforeseen accident or because the worker was not acting with duty of care.

When it comes to your case, you need to prove that a worker: 1) had a duty of care towards your child, 2) this duty of care was breached, and 3) the breach of duty of care resulted in your child's injury. If you can prove these things, you will likely have a strong negligence claim.

In addition to or in place of a negligence claim, you could make a liability claim. You could make a liability claim if your child's injuries were the result of a damaged or defective ride. In this situation, the owner or the maintenance team would be liable for the injuries, since they did not make sure that the equipment was safe.

In order to have a liability claim, the product has to be defective in some way. The elements that a liability claim must have are that your child suffered a loss and was injured, the product or ride was defective or damaged in some way, the defect was what caused their injury, and your family followed all the rules and rode on the ride as it was intended. If your child suffers an injury on a ride that was not a foreseeable injury, and was due to a damaged or defective part, you may likely have a good liability claim.

When someone goes on an amusement park ride, they are usually aware that there are risks of injury when riding. However, if there is a safety belt that doesn't fasten or a safety bar with a screw missing, the rider cannot assume the risk of injury from the faulty rides, since they do not know about them. Damages and defects to the ride are not part of the foreseeable risk, unless the rider is warned about them.

If a staff member at the park is responsible for the accident, they could be legally held liable for your child's injury. However, another factor that you need to take into consideration is the amusement park waiver. Waivers can impact who is held responsible for an accident in the eyes of the law.

Many people get injured every day, and many personal injury cases that occur in the summer months happen at amusement parks, waterparks, and fairs or carnivals. Many times people get injured at these places and think that they have no case and it is not even worth it to call an attorney because they signed a waiver. Some parks have their guests sign a liability waiver so that they are not responsible. Or, liability information is located in the fine print of tickets. But sometimes it does not matter if a waiver was signed, because there may be things that it does not cover.

If injuries occur at these types of places, it is important to hold whoever is at fault responsible for the accident. Reported accidents and lawsuits can make parks change some of their safety precautions, be more careful about preventing injuries, and make them pay compensation for injuries.

A liability waiver is a document that someone signs that acknowledges their understanding of the risks of an activity that they are going to participate in. Some activities like bungee jumping, skydiving, or trampoline parks have people sign a piece of paper when they arrive. Many amusement parks and carnivals simply have the limitations of liability on the back of the ticket. Therefore, you may be agreeing to the risks of the park or carnival without even realizing it. Buying the ticket is essentially in place of you signing a physical waiver.

Many people who get injured at an amusement park or carnival believe that because of the liability waiver, they cannot sue a park for sustaining injuries. Liability waivers are often broad and try to cover just about everything so that the park cannot be responsible for someone getting injured. However, there are some limits to what they can actually waive liability for. Also, each and every amusement ride injury entails a different story, set of circumstances, and injuries from the next, so you should not just assume that the park cannot be held responsible.

One example of how a park might not be liable for an injury is if an older man with heart problems knowingly goes on a roller coaster that has a warning sign for medical conditions. If this man rides that roller coaster and has a heart attack on the ride, the park will most likely not be held responsible for that injury occurring.

But, if a child goes on a ride and there is a mechanical error that causes them to fall, it would be difficult for the park to try and claim that they were not responsible. Similarly, if a ride operator is intoxicated while operating a ride and stops the ride short and causes an accident, it would be difficult for the park to claim that they are not responsible.

Even when a liability waiver is signed, it does not mean that an injured rider cannot file a claim against the park. This is because, when you sign a very broad liability waiver and acknowledge the risks, you are not acknowledging the risks of certain specific situations that might be relevant to your case.

Fairs and festivals that pop up around the state during the summer may become a bit more complicated as far as liability. Unlike amusement parks, many of the rides and booths and different activities are owned by independent groups. This situations can make proving liability very complicated, but it can be done with the help of an attorney who knows the situation and injuries of your case.

Although every case is different, these are questions to ask yourself if your child was injured and you do not know if your family has a personal injury case:

Did your child physically injure themselves, or suffer bodily harm?

If your property was damaged, this is not considered personal injury. Personal injury is harm or loss to one's body. For example, personal injury is if your child lost an arm or broke a rib. In some circumstances, personal injury can also be emotional pain, for example, if your child suffered PTSD or some psychological trauma.

In the case of an amusement park ride accident, if your child was ejected from a ride or fell out of the ride, but was not injured, it is not a personal injury situation. Also, if your child was in a ride accident and a piece of metal flew off of the ride but did not hit the child, this is not personal injury, because the accident did not cause an injury.

Was your child's injury caused by someone else's negligence or the malfunction of something?

Negligence means that someone who was responsible for doing something, did not do it or was being careless. If the person in question failed to act with the level of care that a reasonable person is expected to act with under the circumstances, they are liable. Negligence claims can be established by proving that the person in question had a legal duty of care, failed to perform that duty, this failure of duty was the cause for the injury, and the harm or damage done could be remedied by compensation.

Example: A carnival worker had the legal duty to pay attention to to the ride they were operating and stop the ride at the end. The worker failed to stop the ride at the end because he was texting. Because he did not stop the ride, several riders were injured when they crashed into the riders in front of them. This resulted in whiplash and a concussion for your child. In this case, compensation to your family would help pay medical bills.

Could the harm that your child suffered be remedied by money?

Harm that could be remedied could include: medical bills, suffering from physical and emotional pain, disability accommodations, decreased quality of life. If money could help with the situation that your family is in, it might be a good idea to file a personal injury claim.

Criminal vs. Civil Case

If your child has been injured and you think your family may have a personal injury case or another type of legal issue, you may have questions about the case and the legal system in general. One important question is, what is the difference between criminal cases and civil cases? This is a good question, and there are several key distinctions to understand.

Criminal cases are usually cases that involve someone committing a felony or a misdemeanor. These offenses are crimes against the state, and the state has the ability to charge and prosecute someone for them. Civil cases are usually disagreements between people or parties about property, legal duty, or responsibility. These types of cases are typically resolved with restoration, rather than punishment. A personal injury case is considered a civil case.

The type of punishment is different between criminal and civil cases. In criminal cases, punishment could include fines, probation, and jail time. The purpose of punishment in criminal court is to keep society safe from violence and threats, as well as to deter future crime by punishing those who are responsible. For civil cases, the defendant cannot be held criminally responsible, and therefore, cannot serve jail time. The punishment in civil cases is compensating for damages that were done. Even though a person caused harm, in a personal injury situation, they did not do it on purpose. They should therefore be punished for their negligence, not for a criminal act.

Crimes that are committed are charged and prosecuted by the state. When someone commits a felony, such as robbery, the robbery is considered to be a crime against the state and society. Therefore, a prosecutor charges the individual on behalf of the state. On the other hand, civil cases are filed by the individual who suffered damages, injuries, or loss. This individual is the plaintiff who brings the case to the court, and the defendant is the person who is allegedly responsible for the loss. In criminal cases, it is the prosecutor who files charges and in civil cases, the plaintiff files a case. Is the responsibility of the plaintiff and their attorney to file charges and prove that the defendant is at fault.

The standard for proof is also very different depending on a criminal or civil case. The standard of proof for criminal cases is "beyond a reasonable doubt". This means that the prosecutor must prove to the judge or jury that the defendant committed the crime charged without any doubt. The standard is so high in these cases because the consequences of a criminal record and punishments are so severe. This standard attempts to leave as little room for false conviction as possible. The standard of proof for civil cases is "preponderance of evidence", meaning that it is more likely than not that the defendant is responsible for the alleged offense.

The right to an attorney differs between the two cases. In criminal cases, everyone who is charged with a crime is entitled to an attorney. If the person cannot afford to hire an attorney, the state is required to provide them one. In civil cases, neither the plaintiff, nor the defendant are entitled to an attorney. Both sides are responsible for hiring their own attorney. Sometimes a person's insurance company will provide an attorney on behalf of the company.

In criminal cases, many of the protections given to the defendant by the Constitution are not afforded to the defendant in civil cases. For example, defendants in civil cases are not afforded the rights to representation or the protection from unreasonable searches and seizures.

Filing a Claim

If you think that someone else is at fault for your child's injury and you want to file a claim, here are some steps that you can take. Keep in mind that consulting with an attorney can make this process easier for your family. You can always contact my office for further assistance.

As I've already mentioned, once your child is injured, see a doctor and have them document a treatment plan, diagnosis, physical therapy, and medications. It is important for your child to see a doctor for an injury or pain that they may be experiencing from the accident. Take note of all expenses that you pay for doctor visits, therapy, medications, etc. This is important so that you can prove the financial hardships from your child's injury and get compensation for your bills.

If you decide that you would like to make a claim, consult an attorney that handles personal injury cases and hire one to represent you on your case. You should especially hire an attorney if your family is suffering significant hardships or decreased quality of life.

After hiring an attorney, you will need to discuss all aspects of the case, collect evidence, and decide to either settle out of court or file a lawsuit. At this stage, it will be helpful to collect all medical bills and payments that you have made, collect any names of witnesses, pictures of injuries and accident site, and notes that were taken about the incident.

Your attorney will make a demand of money, either once your child has completed treatment or before they complete treatment. The benefit of waiting to make a demand until after your child has completed medical treatment, is that you will be able to make the maximum demand possible, because you will know all expenses paid. The benefit of making a demand before completing treatment is that you will be able to be compensated and get help paying the bills sooner. Either way, your attorney will evaluate all the evidence of the case and your individual situation and make a recommendation.

Once your attorney makes a demand against the person or party in question, that person may either hire an attorney or defend themself. At this stage, negotiating the amount of money will take place and if an agreement cannot be reached, your attorney can file a lawsuit. During this stage, both attorneys or sides can collect evidence, statements, and witness testimonies.

In a personal injury case, there are two ways to reach the conclusion of the case, and get the desired outcome for injuries, which is compensation. Compensation can be achieved by both parties reaching an agreement. An agreement would require the victim and the insurance company of the defendant to decide on a claim value. This agreement is called a settlement, and it occurs out of court. A settlement essentially means that the responsible party is agreeing to pay for loss or damages, but does not have to go before a judge or admit guilt in the case.

On the other hand, when a claim value cannot be determined, and the insurance company and victim cannot agree on an amount of compensation, further action can be taken. For example, if the defendant does not believe that they are guilty of anything and is not responsible, they may not agree to paying any amount. Another possibility is that the defendant believes that they are responsible but does not agree with the amount of money that the victim is claiming for losses.

The next step in the process, if a settlement cannot be reached, is filing a lawsuit. Any personal injury victim has the right to file a lawsuit. When a lawsuit is filed with the court by the victim's attorney, it is stating who is involved, and what the legal basis is for the lawsuit. The claim will state the dollar amount that is being requested as compensation for loss and injury. The plaintiff can reach this amount while still getting treated and recovering from injury or wait until they are done with treatment, and have a more accurate amount of money to request.

The defendant is then served with the complaint and has a certain time limit to respond. If the defendant does not respond to the complaint within this time, usually it is about 30 days, an automatic judgement will be made on the case. If the defendant responds, they can continue to try and come to an agreement and settle the case.

If an agreement still cannot be reached on a settlement, the case can go to trial or the case can be dismissed based on the legal basis of the claim or a judge's summary decision. If the case goes to trial, the facts and evidence are brought forth and a decision will be made for both parties by a judge. If your child has been injured at an amusement park, waterpark, or carnival and you need assistance with your case, call and speak with an attorney.

This list may seem daunting or confusing, but rest assured, hiring a personal injury lawyer will make the process a lot less intimidating. An attorney will prepare, give recommendations, and be an advocate for you during a difficult time. Again, this list is a general list of stages for a typical personal injury case, but every case is different. Your case may happen a little differently than the steps mentioned above, but this can give you an idea of what to be prepared for.

Common Defenses

If you file a personal injury claim against an amusement park, the park may try to use certain defenses. If this happens, don't panic. It is natural for the park to put up a fight, but if you have solid evidence, you can still get compensation. Here are some of the common defenses that a park may use to undermine your case.

First, the park can say that by using the ride, your child assumed the risk of getting hurt. When your child decided to get onto a ride, they were assuming the possibility that they could be injured. However, you are not assuming the risk that there is a malfunction of the ride, a mechanical error, or that the operator of the ride is not paying attention. If one of these things happened, this defense won't work for the other party.

If your child was injured because of a ride malfunction, this is not considered risk that you were assuming before putting your child on the ride. Therefore, this defense would most likely not hold up in court. In this case, it is the park's job to either have the malfunctions and mechanical errors fixed, or make the riders aware of these issues, before they get on the ride. If the operator is not paying attention and an injury results, this may be considered negligence.

Second, the park may claim that the reason for injury was because of noncompliance with safety rules and regulations. For example, they could say that the reason your child got injured was because they did not follow height and weight requirements or because they stood up on a ride. As long as your child was not breaking any of the rules on the ride, this defense most likely cannot be used. If your child's injury occurred because of them not following the rules, it still could be the park's fault if the rules were not posted for everyone to see.

Third, the park could claim that there was fine print on the admission ticket that you purchased. If there was a disclaimer at the bottom or back side of the ticket, it may state that the park is not liable or at fault for any injury that is sustained on their rides. This claim is usually not taken seriously in lawsuits, however. Disclaimers on tickets usually do not hold up, especially when a child is injured. Children most likely do not understand what liability is. Unfortunately, amusement parks try to put these disclaimers on tickets in order to not have any fault fall to them. This can cause those who do get injured to believe that there is nothing they can do about it, and end up not getting compensation or anything for wrongful injuries. However, even if you realize there was a waiver of liability on the ticket, you should talk to an attorney and see if you still have a case.

Damages and Compensation

The legal term "damages" refers to costs of an injury that was suffered in a personal injury case. If you believe that your child's injury was the result of someone else's action or inaction, you will need to file a claim if you want to take legal action and receive compensation for the injury. A claim is not always easy to calculate, because you are not just filing for the hospital bill when your child got injured. Damages can include their medical bills, medications, physical therapy, etc. Below is a list of different things that may be considered damages.

Out-of-pocket expenses would include ambulance bills, hospital bills, doctors, therapy, medications, medical supplies, in-home care, traveling for medical reasons, and more. There would also be other factors like loss of wages, future losses, and decreased earning capacity. Any expenses that you would normally not be paying had your child not been injured would be included as out-of-pocket expenses that could be factored in.

Out-of-pocket expenses may be easier to calculate than calculating physical losses. Physical losses could include pain and suffering, disabilities, decreased capacity of life, your family's losses, future pain and suffering, and future disability. Along with this, losses to body parts could contribute to damages. This would include loss of limbs, specifically your child's dominant hand or arm, entire leg, just leg below the knee, loss of foot, and amputation to both arms or both legs. Other damages could be damage to your child's back or neck, or brain damage.

Some questions may be important in calculating your child's physical losses or when presenting the injury case at trial in front of a judge. First, what kind of pain did your child feel and experience during the accident? Second, what kind of pain did your child feel while recovering from the accident, or that they still currently have? Next, did your child's injury cause them to experience trauma, anxiety, PTSD, depression, loss of enjoyment in life, etc.?

Another question to think about is if your child had any hobbies or activities that they can no longer do or if they now cause pain due to the injuries. Examples of this would be sports, cooking, playing an instrument, gardening, etc. Lastly, does your loved one struggle with day-to-day functions like driving, cooking, laundry, doing the dishes, etc.?

The purpose of this guide to calculating your child's damages and questions to ask is to get an idea about the kinds of things that you will need to consider when pursuing a personal injury case. This guide is just a general overview, and does not include every single factor that can be considered. The best way to fully and accurately estimate your family's damages is to consult with an attorney. If your child has been injured in a waterpark, amusement park, or carnival, consult with an attorney so you can get professional help with filing a claim for damages.

CONCLUSION

We hope that this book has answered your questions about amusement park injuries. If you have a loved one who was injured at an amusement park, waterpark, or similar place, you now have the tools to seek help.

While this book is a good starting point for learning about personal injury, chances are it has not answered every question that you have. Each case is different, and this book is only meant to be used as a general overview. If you are seeking more detailed information for your child's situation, please contact our office. We are happy to go over your situation, answer questions, and help determine the best way for your family to seek justice. You can reach us at 888-487-8543 for more information.

Made in the USA
Monee, IL
04 November 2026

67385838R10075